南 無 本 師 釋 迦 牟 尼 佛
NAMO FUNDAMENTAL TEACHER SHAKYAMUNI BUDDHA

觀音菩薩也不一定是男身，也不一定是女身；
他也是男身，也是女身，不過都是變化的。
那麼觀音菩薩的本體呢？
他是如如不動的，和佛一樣。

Guanyin Bodhisattva is not necessarily male or female.

He is both male and female, but that's just his transformation.

In his fundamental identity,

Guanyin Bodhisattva is thus and unmoving,

just like the Buddhas.

觀世音菩薩不是中國人，也不是外國人，
他是哪兒的人呢？他是盡虛空遍法界，
哪個地方都是他，哪個地方也都不是他。

Guanyin Bodhisattva is neither Chinese

nor any other nationality.

Where is he from then?

He can be found everywhere throughout space

and the Dharma Realm, and yet there is no place where he is.

現在菩提種子已經播種在西方，正在發芽生長中，
不久的將來，就會開菩提花，結菩提果。

The seeds of Bodhi have already been sown in the West,

And now it is time for them to sprout and grow.

In the near future they will blossom and bear Bodhi fruit.

「行如風，坐如鐘，臥如弓，立如松」，
這四大威儀是日常生活中要注意的儀態。
"Walk like the breeze, sit like a bell,
recline like a bow, and stand like a pine."
We should pay attention to the
Four Modes of Deportment in our daily lives.

大教育家——孔子，
他雖然置身橫逆之境，
仍不改變教育宗旨。
Confucius—A Great Educator
Even though he constantly faced setbacks,
he never altered his principles of education.

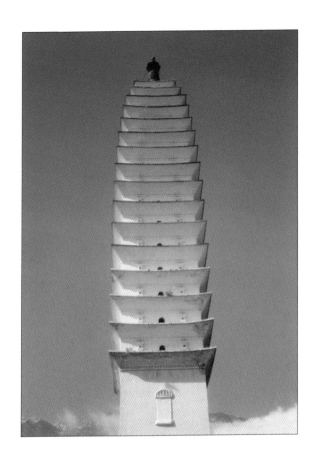

一座寶塔，無論多高多大，必須從地上建起。
菩提心，也是從心地上建起，愈發愈大，愈發愈高。
No matter how tall a pagoda you plan to build,
You have to start from the ground.
The Bodhi resolve is similarly built up from the mind ground.
Starting very small, it gradually grows greater and higher.

書到用時方恨少，
事非經過不知難。

Only at the time of actual application
do you realize that your knowledge is limited;
Not until you've tried something
do you know the difficulties involved.

凡事「擇善而從，不善而改。」
　　「是道則進，非道則退。」

We should always choose to follow good examples

and change conduct that is not virtuous.

"If it's the Way, advance upon it;

if it's not the Way, retreat from it."

「老吾老以及人之老」，
我們不但要孝順自己的父母，
也要孝順他人的父母。

Be filial not only to your own parents,
but to the parents of others as well. It is said,
"Care for your own elders and
extend the same care to the elders of others."

「幼吾幼，以及人之幼」，
我們不單慈愛自己的子女，
也要慈愛他人的子女。

Love not only your own children,

but the children of others as well. It is said,

"Look after your own children and

extend the same concern to the children of others."

我們活著為什麼？

這個「我」是誰？是你、是我，也是他；

可是我們來到這個世界，又為了什麼呢？

What are we living for?

Who are we?

What are we here for?

世間法就好像一個大羅網，把所有人都網住了。
愛名的便被名網所網，
貪財的便被財網所纏，
迷色的便被色網所縛。

Worldly affairs are like a huge net that binds people up.

Fame-seekers are bound by the net of fame;

Money-worshippers get caught in the net of wealth;

And promiscuous individuals are trapped in the net of lust.

有子強如父，留財做什麼？
有子不如父，留錢做什麼？

If the son is more capable than the father,

What need is there to leave him wealth?

If the son is weaker than the father,

What's the use of leaving him money?

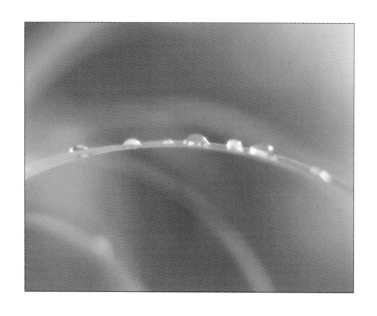

一切有為法，如夢幻泡影，
如露亦如電，應作如是觀。

All worldly phenomena
Are like dreams, illusions, bubbles,
and shadows;
Like dew and like lightning.
We should contemplate them thus.

宣化上人德相

The Venerable Master Hsuan Hua

宣化上人開示錄

（九）

Venerable Master Hua's
Talks on Dharma

Volume Nine

宣化上人開示錄

（九）

佛經翻譯委員會

英　譯

法界佛教總會
佛經翻譯委員會
法界佛教大學
出　版

Venerable Master Hua's
Talks on Dharma

Volume Nine

English translation by the
Buddhist Text Translation Society

Buddhist Text Translation Society
Dharma Realm Buddhist University
Dharma Realm Buddhist Association
Burlingame, California U.S.A.

宣化上人開示錄（九）
Venerable Master Hua's Talks on Dharma
Volume Nine

Published and translated by:
Buddhist Text Translation Society
1777 Murchison Drive,
Burlingame, CA 94010-4504

© 2001   **Buddhist Text Translation Society**
Dharma Realm Buddhist University
Dharma Realm Buddhist Association

First Chinese edition published 1984,
Dharma Realm Buddhist Books Distribution Society, as
宣化上人開示錄（五）、（六）
(hsüan hua shang ren kai shi lu—wu, liu)

First bilingual edition 2001
(Fifth Chinese edition, First English edition)
04 03 02 01   10 9 8 7 6 5 4 3 2 1

ISBN 0-88139-858-6
Library of Congress Catalog Card Number: 96-136258

Printed in Taiwan

Note: Pinyin is used for the romanization of Chinese words,
        except for proper names which retain familiar romanizations.

佛經翻譯委員會八項基本守則
The Eight Guidelines of
The Buddhist Text Translation Society

1. 從事翻譯工作者不得抱有個人的名利。
   A volunteer must free him/herself from the motives of personal fame and profit.

2. 從事翻譯工作者不得貢高我慢，必須以虔誠恭敬的態度來工作。
   A volunteer must cultivate a respectful and sincere attitude free from arrogance and conceit.

3. 從事翻譯工作者不得自讚毀他。
   A volunteer must refrain from aggrandizing his/her work and denigrating that of others.

4. 從事翻譯工作者不得自以為是，對他人作品吹毛求疵。
   A volunteer must not establish him/herself as the standard of correctness and suppress the work of others with his or her fault-finding.

5. 從事翻譯工作者必須以佛心為己心。
   A volunteer must take the Buddha-mind as his/her own mind.

6. 從事翻譯工作者必須運用擇法眼來辨別正確的道理。
   A volunteer must use the wisdom of Dharma-Selecting Vision to determine true principles.

7. 從事翻譯工作者必須懇請十方大德長老來印證其翻譯。
   A volunteer must request Virtuous Elders in the ten directions to certify his/her translations.

8. 從事翻譯工作者之作品在獲得印證之後，必須努力弘揚流通經、律、論以及佛書以光大佛教。
   A volunteer must endeavor to propagate the teachings by printing Sutras, Shastra texts, and Vinaya texts when the translations are certified as being correct.

目　錄

CONTENTS

兒童是國家的棟樑

現在就要把救國救民的基礎打堅固，
首先要學做好人。

各位小朋友！把身挺直直的，靜心坐在禪凳上，我
今天要對你們說幾句話。你們好像小樹，一天比一
天長高，將來可作棟樑之材。你們將來是國家的棟
樑，要做一番轟轟烈烈的大事業，爲世界求和平，
爲人類謀幸福。你們生在這個國家（美國），就應
該把這個國家治理得好好的，使這個國家沒有戰爭
，永遠平安，乃至使全世界所有的國家，都得到平
安，這是你們的責任。

現在就要把救國救民的基礎打堅固，首先要學做好
人，即是向好人學習，不要學壞人。什麼是好人？

Children Are the Supporting Pillars of a Nation

Now is the time to build a solid foundation in order to save the country and the people.
First of all you must learn to be a good person.

Young friends, sit upright on your meditation cushions and calm your minds. I want to say a few words to you today. You are just like young trees growing taller day by day, and in the future you will become pillars of support. You are the future supporting pillars of your country. You should do great things and work for world peace and the welfare of humankind. Since you are born in this country, you should help manage and govern this country so that there will be no wars and life will always be secure and peaceful. Then you should extend your effort so that all the countries of this world will also have peace. That is your duty.

Now is the time to build a solid foundation in order to save the country and the people. First of all you must learn to be a good person. This means learning from good people, not from bad ones. Who is a good person? A person who is filial

3

就是在家中孝順父母，在學校恭敬師長，在社會爲人群服務，在政府爲民謀幸福，這是好人的標準。什麼是壞人？就是自私自利、見利忘義的人。好人治理國家，使國家能富強而無戰爭；壞人治理國家，能令國家滅亡。

你們是這個國家的先覺者，因爲你們知道盡孝道，知道爲人服務，將來要將國家治理得平平安安，把殺人的武器，統統消滅，所謂「馬放南山，刀鎗入庫。」你們的責任，是要化解這世界戰爭的戾氣，使人人都能安居樂業，豐衣足食，這樣世界就能成爲大同世界。

一九八三年八月二十日開示於萬佛聖城

to his parents at home, respects his teachers at school, serves the people in society, and works for the welfare of the people when serving in the government. Those are the standards of a good person. Who is a bad person? A person who is selfish and self-benefiting, and who forgets justice when he sees a chance to benefit himself. Under the government of good people a nation will become affluent, strong and peaceful. But if managed by bad people, the nation will collapse.

In this country, you are more conscious than others, since you know about filiality and know how to work for and serve the people. In the future, you can manage this country so that it is safe and peaceful. Destroy all lethal weapons. It is said, "The horses are set free on the south mountain, and weapons are stored in the warehouse." Your responsibility is to dissolve the violent energy of wars in the world, and to allow the people to live securely and happily, well-fed and well-clothed. Then the world will be one of great harmony.

A talk given on August 12, 1983,
at the City of Ten Thousand Buddhas

何謂敦品，何謂立德

要時時將不正的枝椏砍去，
令其向上發展，將來成為大樹，
可做有用的大材料。

小朋友！你們想盡救世救人的責任嗎？首先要「敦品立德」。

何謂敦品？「敦」是敦厚；「品」是品格，就是要學識豐富，品格高尚，不吸菸、不飲酒、更不吸毒、不賭錢，完全沒有不良的嗜好。不要學過去那些無知識的人，對國家不負責任，對社會不盡義務，隨隨便便不守規矩，成為害群之馬，人間的阿修羅，只知鬥爭，不知和平，這種惡人只會成為國家的大包袱。

6

On Developing Good Character and Virtue

Constantly trim the crooked branches so the trunk can grow upright; become a big tree that's useful material for the future.

Young friends! Do you want to fulfill the responsibility of saving the people and the world? Then first of all, you should develop good character and virtue.

What does it mean to develop good character? If you want to be a person of learning and integrity, then don't smoke, drink, take drugs, or gamble; be free of all bad habits. Don't learn from ignorant people who aren't responsible to their country, who don't fulfill their duties in society, who are careless and don't observe the rules. They are the black sheep of the flock and *asuras* in the human realm. They know only about fighting, not about peace. Those kinds of unwholesome people will merely become a great burden for the nation.

你們現在正像欣欣向榮的小樹，要時時將不正的枝椏砍去，令其向上發展，將來成為大樹，可做有用的大材料。所謂「十年樹木，百年樹人。」你們現在正是學習的時期，不要沾染種種的不良習氣。切記！養成高尚的品格，保持廉潔的操守。若能這樣，將來能作世界人類的領袖。

何謂立德？「立」是建立，「德」是德行。建立好的德行，也就是孝順父母，所謂「百善孝為先」。不孝順父母的人，就是天天拜佛，也沒有用處。關於這一點，小朋友！要特別注意。

你們的德行，一天比一天多起來；做人的基礎，一天比一天堅固。該說話的時候，要說正當如理的話，不說不合理的話。總而言之，你們要努力學習，將來成為世界上有用的人，不可做世界上的壞人。這是我對你們的期望。

Now you are just like young, flourishing trees. Your crooked branches must constantly be trimmed so that the trunks can grow upright. Then you can become great trees, providing useful lumber in the future. It is said, "It takes ten years to grow a tree, but a hundred years to educate a person." You are now in the learning phase. Don't get defiled by bad habits. Remember to cultivate an honorable character and maintain honest conduct. Then you can be leaders in the world.

How do you build virtue? Be filial to your parents. It is said, "Among the hundred good deeds, filiality is the foremost." People who aren't filial to their parents will be useless even if they bow to the Buddha every day. You should pay close attention to this, young friends!

Your virtue is increasing day by day, and your foundation for being a person is getting more solid day by day. When it's time to talk, you should say proper and decent things, not improper things. You should always study hard and become a productive person in the future, not a bad person. That is my expectation for you.

萬佛聖城義務教育

教育良才，是人生最快樂的事。

萬佛聖城成立育良小學、培德中學、法界佛教大學，一律免收學費，成為義務教育。我告訴你們不收學費的因緣。

我的家住在東北雙城縣的山中，交通不大方便，村中又沒有學校，所以兒童多數失學，村民大多數是文盲。在我十五歲那年的秋天，才入私塾讀書，讀四書五經。到十七歲那年冬天，我把四書五經讀完，老師隨我所讀，便為我講解書中的義理，一共讀了兩年半的書。

Free Education at the City of Ten Thousand Buddhas

Teaching is the greatest joy in life.

Dharma Realm Buddhist University, Developing Virtue Secondary School, and Instilling Goodness Elementary School at the City of Ten Thousand Buddhas are all tuition-free and offer free education. Let me tell you the reason we don't charge tuition.

My family lived in the mountains of Shuangcheng County in Manchuria. Since public transportation was inadequate and there was no school in the village, most children didn't go to school and most of the villagers were illiterate. When I was fifteen years old, I went to an old-style private school to study the Four Books and the Five Classics. I finished studying them in the winter of my seventeenth year. As I studied those books, the teacher would explain them to me. It took me two and a half years to finish.

我到十八歲的時候，無書可讀，就輟學在家，研究醫術書籍，大約讀了十五、六本，明白「望、聞、問、切」的道理，知道「寒、熱、溫、平」的藥性，可以治病，但是就不給人家看病，因爲我總覺得在一百個病人之中，縱能治好九十九個病人，只有一個病人的病，或者下錯藥，或者誤醫，還是有罪過，所以沒打算以行醫爲業，又兼我一向對錢不重視，一直到現在，仍是這樣。

在這一年之中，我又看了相面的書，爻卦的書，批八字的書，算命的書，我對於醫卜星相等書，雖然不算精通，可是皆明白其理，不過，我也沒有做這種種行業，因爲我不想賺錢，我常想「富貴花間露，功名瓦上霜」，都是無常。

是年的冬天，我見村中的兒童沒有機會讀書，實在可憐，乃發心成立義學，不收任何人的學費。當時有三十多個學生，由我一人擔任教學。因爲學生的年齡不同，智慧不同，所以採取個別教學的方法。從早晨七點鐘開始上課，下午六時下課，在這中間

When I was eighteen, there were no books at school for me to study, so I stayed home and read Chinese medicine texts, about fifteen or sixteen of them. I learned to distinguish the nature of medicinal herbs as being cold, hot, warm, or mild, and understood how to diagnose a patient by observing them, asking questions, taking their pulse, and listening to them. I could have treated patients, but I didn't, because I always felt that if I gave a wrong diagnosis or prescribed the wrong medicine in one case out of a hundred, then even if I successfully cured the other ninety-nine, I would still have an offense. That's why I never wanted to be a doctor. Also, I have never cared about money, even to this day.

During the same year, I also read some books on physiognomy, divination, the eight hexagrams, and similar subjects. I was not an expert in those subjects, but I understood the principles involved. However, I did not take them up as a profession, because I didn't want to make money. I always thought of how "wealth is like morning dew on the flowers, and fame is like frost on the roof tiles." They are both impermanent.

That winter, I saw that the village children had no access to education. It was really pitiful. I decided to start a free school. There were about thirty students, and I was the only teacher. Since the students were of different ages and levels of intelligence, I tutored them individually. The school opened from seven o'clock in the morning till six o'clock in the evening, with no break in between. The students all studied very hard and made quick progress. When school ended after the winter, the students showed considerable

沒有休息時間。學生認真學習，進步很快。冬天過去，學校結束了，學生的成績很好，認識了很多字，也會寫很多字，這是我辛苦換來的代價。

所以育良小學、培德中學、法界佛教大學，也不收學費。有人懷疑，是不是太愚癡？不知錢好用？的確愚癡到極點，我承認這種評論，但我有個構想，教育良才，是人生最快樂的事。

育良小學：旨在教育世界優良的人才，教育世界良善的國民，教育世界盡善的孝子，所以叫作育良。

培德中學：因為人的本來德性不能圓滿具足，所以要栽培德行，提倡修福修慧。育良小學注重孝道，所謂「百善孝為先」。培德中學注重忠孝，忠於國家，孝順父母。愛護自己的國家，作為良善的公民，必須先把人格建立堅固，才經得起考驗。不向環境投降，所謂「家貧出孝子，亂世出忠臣」，這都是經得起考驗。有高尚的人格，有偉大的志願，有堅忍不拔、百折不撓的精神，有能做一番轟轟烈烈的大事業，這是培德中學的目標。

achievement. They had learned to read and write many characters. That was the reward for my hard work.

The schools at the City are also tuition-free. Some people may wonder: "Are you people so stupid that you don't know how useful money can be?" Yes, it is extremely stupid, I have to admit. But I have this idea that teaching is the greatest joy in life.

Instilling Goodness Elementary School: The goal is to develop students' talents and potential, teaching them to be good citizens and perfectly filial children. That's why the school is called "Instilling Goodness."

Developing Virtue Secondary School: Since people are not born with perfect and complete virtue, we should help them to develop virtue and to cultivate both blessings and wisdom. Instilling Goodness Elementary School focuses on filiality. It is said, "Among the hundred good deeds, filiality is foremost." Developing Virtue Secondary School emphasizes loyalty and filiality—loyalty to one's country and filiality to one's parents. In order to protect one's own country and be a good citizen, one must first establish a strong character and be able to endure tests without succumbing to circumstances. It is said, "Filial sons come from poor families; loyal officials are produced from national turmoil." This describes people who can endure tests. With a noble character, great resolve, and a persevering and indomitable spirit, one can achieve great things. This is the aim of Developing Virtue Secondary School.

法界佛教大學：學生在培德中學把德行栽培圓滿，進入法界佛教大學深造，成為出乎其類、拔乎其萃的人才。希望你們能青出於藍，而勝於藍，將來到社會成為頂天立地的奇男子或奇女人。要有人溺己溺，人飢己飢的思想。這種抱負要盡虛空遍法界，永不變更。

現在多數的學校，無論公立或私立，專在學生身上打主意，學費年年提高，令無錢的子弟，有望洋興嘆之感。萬佛聖城為解決這個難題，所以不收學費，以教育天下英才為宗旨。我希望在萬佛聖城受教育的學生，知道萬佛聖城用心良苦，乃是犧牲大量經費，教育你們成為國的棟樑，弘法的人才。你們不要辜負萬佛聖城培育之苦心，要用功讀書，所謂

> 書到用時方恨少，
> 事非經過不知難。

你們現在如果不用功，將來到用時就後悔了。這是我今天要對你們說的話。

一九八三年九月十九日

Dharma Realm Buddhist University: After students have perfected their virtue in Developing Virtue Secondary School, they may enter Dharma Realm Buddhist University to further their studies and become outstanding people. I hope you will surpass your teachers and become preeminent men and women in society. Your attitude should be: "When I see others drowning, it is as if I am drowning; when I see others starving, it is as if I am starving." This ideal should pervade space and the Dharma Realm and never change.

Nowadays most schools, both public and private, constantly scheme to make a profit off the students. Tuition increases every year, which frustrates the children of less affluent families. The City solves this problem by not collecting any tuition and taking the development of students' talents as its goal. I hope the students here will understand the sincere intentions of the City. We spend a lot of money to educate you so that in the future you may become pillars of society who are capable of propagating the Dharma. Study hard and don't disappoint the expectations placed upon you by the City of Ten Thousand Buddhas. It is said,

> Only at the time of actual application
>   do you realize that your knowledge is limited;
> Not until you've tried something
>   do you know the difficulties involved.

If you don't study hard now, you will regret it when it's time to put your knowledge to use. That's what I wanted to say to you today.

A talk given on September 19, 1983

一切放下真自在

好和不好都能覺悟，便沒有問題了。

這世界上無論好和不好，都是教人覺悟。好，就是
教你覺悟好的地方；不好，就是教你覺悟不好的地
方。好和不好都能覺悟，便沒有問題了。若好的不
覺悟，便執著在這個好上；不好的不覺悟，便執著
在一個不好上。無論執著「好」或「不好」，都是
一種執著，有這種執著，在道業上就不能有所成就
。必須要把好和不好的都看破，順境逆境都能處之
泰然，就可以不被境界所轉。《金剛經》上說：

　　　一切有爲法，如夢幻泡影，
　　　如露亦如電，應作如是觀。

Let Go of Everything and Gain True Freedom!

If we awaken to both the good and the bad, there is no problem.

Everything in the world, both good and bad, is telling us to wake up. Good things help us wake up to the positive aspect of things; bad things make us aware of the negative side of things. If we awaken to both the good and the bad, there is no problem. If we don't wake up to the good, we'll be attached to good things. Likewise, if we aren't aware of the bad, we'll be attached to bad things. Either way, we will have attachments and be unable to realize the Way. We must see through both good and bad, and be at ease in both favorable and adverse situations. We shouldn't be affected by external circumstances. The *Vajra Sutra* says:

> All worldly phenomena
> Are like dreams, illusions, bubbles, and shadows;
> Like dew and like lightning.
> We should contemplate them thus.

世間上一切有爲法，好像作夢一樣，並不眞實。又好像水中的浮泡一樣，是不實在的。也像影子一樣，看是有，卻捉不住。又如同露水、雷電，瞬息消逝。應作這樣觀察，才能眞正地看破；看破之後，還要放下。如果放不下，執著這個，執著那個，便得不到自在。無論順境或是逆境，把它放下，毫不執著，才能得到自在。

一九八〇年九月十日開示

The things of this world are no more real than a dream; they are as ephemeral as bubbles, as intangible as shadows. They are as fleeting as the morning dew and flashes of lighting which disappear in the blink of an eye. Regarding them in this way, we will be able to see through them and let go of them. If we continue clinging to them, we won't be truly free. We should relinquish our attachments to pleasant as well as unpleasant events. We can be truly free only when every last bit of attachment is gone.

A talk given on September 10, 1980

錢能招殺身之禍

錢積集多了，它會害死人。

小朋友！不要想如何升官？如何發財？怎樣能在世界上有名望？怎樣能在國際上出風頭？應該要想怎樣才能爲人類謀幸福，怎樣才能爲人類造利益。我們是幫助世界和平，幫助眾生安樂。不是在世界上爭名奪利，勾心鬥角，互相陷害。若是爲目的而不擇手段，就是造罪業。

錢積集多了，它會害死人。最近洛杉磯發生一件富人被害的新聞。這個財主（美國人），很有錢，但行爲放蕩不羈，因爲錢財的糾紛，被人害死。他活

Money Can Kill You

Accumulating wealth can be lethal.

Young friends! Don't focus your thoughts on getting a promotion, making money, winning fame in the world, or becoming a world celebrity. Instead, think about how to work for the welfare of human beings, how to benefit humanity. We want to promote world peace and help living beings be happy. We don't want to fight for fame and benefit, or plot against each other. If you get what you want by hook or by crook, you are creating offenses.

Accumulating wealth can be lethal. Recently in Los Angeles, a man was killed. This man was very rich, but he was not careful in his conduct. He was killed due to a conflict over money. Since he was rich, he committed a lot of offenses when he was alive, and that is why he came to such an end.

著的時候，因爲有錢，造了很多罪孽，才有如此的
下場，雖然有萬貫家產，但是帶不去一分錢。各位
想一想！這有什麼價值？有什麼意義？

所以在世界上要作有智慧的人，不要作愚癡的人。
有智慧的人，對於事理分析清清楚楚，對於善惡辨
別明明白白，絕對不做顛倒事。愚癡的人，終日求
名、求利、求地位、求權勢，看不破，放不下，見
利忘義，盡做些虧心的生意，醉生夢死，糊塗一輩
子。我們在這世界上要幫助困苦的人，伸出援手，
拯救他們於水深火熱，所謂「爲善最樂」，這是助
人爲快樂之本。

一九八三年九月二十二日

Although he had property worth millions, he couldn't take a penny with him when he died. Think about it: Is there any meaning in such an existence?

We want to be wise people, not fools. A wise person understands principles, distinguishes clearly between good and evil, and never does deluded things. A fool spends his days chasing after fame and gain, social status, and power. He fails to see their true nature and relinquish his pursuit. He forgets about justice when he sees a chance to benefit himself. He often does things that go against his conscience, and is muddled—as if drunk or dreaming—all his life. We ought to help these pathetic people. We should give them a hand and save them from the deep waters and scorching fires. It is said, "Doing good is the greatest joy in life." Helping others brings happiness.

A talk given on September 22, 1983

建立堅固的基礎

**要知道幫助世界平安，
先要從教育著手。**

萬佛聖城教育的宗旨，是先要把「人格的基礎打好」，令小學生、中學生、大學生，人人皆知「禮義廉恥、忠孝仁愛」的道理。換句話說，注重精神教育。令學生把做人的基礎穩固，將來到社會上做事，本著道德的思想。如此能做人的標準，做人的榜樣，令眾人向你們看齊學習，慢慢的薰染，將社會上不良的風氣，糾正過來，成為夜不閉戶，路不拾遺的境界。

這個世界為什麼不好？因為沒有把做人的基礎打好。所以被「財色名食睡」五欲之風，吹得東倒西歪

Building a Solid Foundation

To promote world peace, we have to start with education.

The first objective of education at the City of Ten Thousand Buddhas is building a good foundation for character, enabling all elementary, secondary, and university students to understand the principles of propriety, righteousness, honesty, a sense of shame, loyalty, filiality, humaneness, and love. In other words, we emphasize educating the mind and spirit, so that the students have a solid foundation for being a person. In the future, when they start working, they will base their actions on virtue and serve as models for others. People will look up to and learn from them, and their influence will gradually reverse the unwholesome trends of society. Then there will be no need to lock the doors at night, and lost articles will always be returned.

Why is the world not doing well? No one has laid a good foundation for humanity. Consequently, people are all

，迷迷糊糊，只知尋求五欲的快樂，不知「孝悌忠信」為何物？不知「仁義禮智信」的道理。所以把世界弄得烏煙瘴氣，不成體統。

萬佛聖城的教育，教人打好地基，將來可建摩天大樓。我就是打地基的大錘，把小朋友的基礎打得堅堅實實，將來作為世界的良材，這是我的目的。小朋友！不要把自己看輕，你們是國家未來的主人翁。你們在課堂中，除了靜心聽老師講解之外，還要訓練演講，有了經驗，養成無所畏的心理，將來成為弘法人才，辯才無礙。

各位老師！你們多辛苦點，將這群有為的青年，訓練成有智慧、有幹勁、見義勇為、奉公守法、優秀的公民。要知道幫助世界平安，先要從教育著手。教育基礎打好，國家定能富強，世界定能和平。現在因為其他國家的教育基礎沒有堅固的緣故，所以造出不守規矩的青年，飽食終日，無所事事，徘徊街頭，成為浪子。

swayed by the winds of the five desires: wealth, sex, fame, food, and sleep. They become muddled, seeking only to gratify those five desires. They have no idea of what filiality, fraternal respect, loyalty, and trustworthiness are. They know nothing about the principles of humaneness, righteousness, propriety, wisdom, and trustworthiness. Therefore the world is chaotic and pervaded with a foul atmosphere.

The education given at the City teaches people to lay a good, solid foundation upon which skyscrapers can be built. I've been the big hammer, hammering our young friends' foundations so that they'll be solid and useful to the world in the future. That is my goal. Young friends, do not underestimate yourselves. You are the future leaders of this country. In the classroom, aside from quietly listening to the teacher's lecture, you must also practice public speaking. After you have gained some experience and are no longer afraid, you will be able to propagate the Dharma with boundless eloquence.

Teachers, please work hard to train these young people to become wise, energetic, law-abiding, model citizens who will never hesitate to do what is right. In order to promote world peace, we have to start with education. As long as we lay down a good foundation in education, the nation will surely be strong and prosperous, and the world will be safe and peaceful. Since some countries don't have a solid educational foundation, they have numerous juvenile delinquents who eat their fill and have nothing better to do than wander in the streets like vagabonds.

我敢說凡是在萬佛聖城受教育的學生，無論是大學生、中學生、小學生，個個都是守規矩的學生，知道怎樣做人，知道怎樣立德。希望你們依此爲方針，努力學習，成爲國家有用的人。

I daresay that students at the City—whether they are in the university, secondary school, or elementary school—are all good students who observe the rules and know how to behave as decent human beings who develop their own virtue. I hope that based on these guidelines, you will work hard and become people who are useful to the nation.

大教育家——孔子

他雖然置身橫逆之境，
仍不改變教育宗旨。

在中國春秋時代有位大聖人出世，就是孔子。他一生極力到處宣揚「仁義道德，孝悌忠信」的學說，可是不受歡迎，處處受排斥。他雖然置身橫逆之境，仍不改變教育宗旨，貫徹始終地提倡大同之道。

孔子是位大教育家，提倡「有教無類」的平民教育，不遺餘力。他有「教不厭，學不倦」的精神。他是一位「述而不作，信而好古」的實行家。孔子晚年刪《詩經》、制「禮樂」、著《春秋》——詩、書、易、禮、春秋，即現在的五經。

Confucius—A Great Educator

Even though he constantly faced setbacks, he never altered his principles of education.

During the Spring and Autumn period [722 – 484 B.C.] of Chinese history, in 551 B.C., a great sage was born. He was Confucius. Throughout his life, he tirelessly propagated the virtues of humaneness and righteousness, and the doctrines of filiality, fraternal respect, loyalty, and trustworthiness. But instead of being welcomed, he was rejected everywhere he went. Even though he constantly faced setbacks, he never altered his principles of education and continued promoting the way of peace and harmony.

Confucius was a great educator. He spared no effort in promoting the idea of equal and universal education. He was "never weary of teaching and never tired of learning." Instead of composing new texts, he explained the ancient books in a faithful and devoted fashion. In his later years, he edited the *Book of Odes*, compiled the rites and music, and

他的學生有三千人，身通禮、樂、射、御、書、數六藝的有七十二人。「禮」是婚喪祭祀的禮節；「樂」是音樂；「射」是射箭；「御」是駕車；「書」是寫字；「數」是算數。必須樣樣精通，才能成爲完人。

孔子的教育方針──「因人施教，以身作則。」他的學生分爲四大科：

（一）德行：有顏回、閔子騫。
（二）言語：有子貢、宰我。
（三）政事：有子路、冉有。
（四）文學：有子夏、子游。

孔子卒後，分爲兩派，曾子主張「傳道」，以孟子代表，後爲正統。子夏主張「傳經」，以荀子爲代表。「傳經派」興於漢唐清三朝代；「傳道派」興於宋元明三朝代。

wrote the *Spring and Autumn Annals*. The *Book of Odes*, the *Book of History*, the *Book of Changes*, the *Book of Rites*, and the *Spring and Autumn Annals* are now known as the Five Classics.

Confucius had three thousand students. Among these there were seventy-two who mastered the six skills of rites, music, archery, charioteering, writing, and mathematics. Rites refer to the proper ceremonial rituals for weddings, funerals, and sacrificial offerings. One has to master all six skills before one can be considered a perfect person.

Confucius taught each person according to his or her individual potential, and he taught by example. His students can be divided into four main categories [according to their area of strength]:

1. Virtue, represented by Yan Hui and Min Ziqian
2. Speech, represented by Zi Gong and Zai Wo
3. Politics, represented by Zi Lu and Ran You
4. Literature, represented by Zi Xia and Zi You

After Confucius' death, his students split into two sects. Zeng Zi advocated the propagation of the Way (Tao); Mencius represented this school, which was later recognized as the orthodoxy. Zi Xia advocated the propagation of classics, and that school was represented by Xun Zi. The school advocating the propagation of classics prevailed during the Han, Tang and Qing dynasties, while the school advocating the propagation of the Way prevailed during the Song, Yuan and Ming dynasties.

世界上的事理，都有相互的關係，好像中國的「儒、道、佛」三教，都是互相幫助。「儒教」如同啓蒙的小學，「道教」如同中學，「佛教」就是大學。三教道理都有關連，可是小學生不知中學的教科書，但是大學生可知中小學的課程。

「儒教」講做人的道理，如何建立好的人格。「道教」一半重於建立好人格，一半是修出世法。所以道士不剃頭髮，與在家人一樣，但穿古時隱士所穿的衣服。「佛教」則剃髮除鬚，穿壞色衣，不注重外表，可是袈裟不離身，現比丘、比丘尼相。佛教是修出世法的道理，是不是離開世間法而另外有佛法？也不是的。只要將世間法認識清楚了，不被其所迷，就是佛法。

有人主張「三教合一」。所謂：

> 紅花白藕青荷葉，
> 三教原來是一家。

這就是表示儒釋道。佛教之根本，發起信仰之肇基

The noumena and phenomena in the world are all interrelated. In China, Confucianism, Taoism and Buddhism have aided each other. Confucianism is like an elementary school for young children, Taoism is like a secondary school, and Buddhism is like a university. The principles of these three religions are related. Students in the elementary school don't understand the subjects taught at the secondary school, but university students know the curriculums of both the elementary and secondary schools.

Confucianism teaches the principles of being a person and developing a wholesome character. Taoism places half its emphasis on establishing a good character and half on the cultivation of transcendental principles. For that reason Taoist priests are like laypeople in that they do not shave their heads; however, they do dress like the hermits of ancient times. Buddhist monks, on the other hand, shave their hair and beard, wear clothes of dark and somber colors, and don't care about their external appearance. They maintain the appearance of Bhikshus and Bhikshunis and always wear their sashes. Buddhism teaches people to cultivate the principles of world-transcending Dharma. Is there a Buddhadharma outside of worldly dharmas? No. As long as you truly recognize worldly dharmas and are not deluded by them, just that is the Buddhadharma.

Some people have suggested combining the three religions into one. It is said,

> Like the red blossom, the white root, and the
>   green leaf of a lotus plant,
> The three religions originate from one family.

，乃是在儒教，必須讀書，明理，先學如何做人，然後再依法修行，所謂「歸元性無二，方便有多門。」學佛法的人，應該懂得這個道理。

一九八三年九月二十五日

This expresses how Confucianism, Buddhism and Taoism are interrelated. The roots of Buddhism, the foundation upon which faith arises, lie within Confucianism. One has to study, understand the principles, and learn how to be a person first, and then one can cultivate in accord with the Dharma. It is said, "Even though there are many expedient doors, the nature at the source is nondual." Students of Buddhism should understand this principle.

A talk given on September 25, 1983

大學之道

這學說，是最基本之理想，
也是儒教所依據之道理。

大學之道以「三綱領」和「八條目」爲宗旨。何謂
三綱領？就是「明德，親民，止於至善。」

（一）明德：自己的德性清淨光明之後，也敎他人
的德性清淨光明。

（二）親民：令所有老百姓知道正當的道路，做個
明理的人。

（三）止於至善：大家居處於最完善的地方。

The Way of Great Learning

These are the fundamental ideas of Confucius' teaching, and also the principles upon which Confucianism is based.

The Way of the Great Learning consists of three guidelines and eight articles. The three guidelines are: illustrating virtue, renewing the people, and resting in the highest excellence.

1. *Illustrating virtue* means that after one's own virtue become pure and bright, one teaches others to make their virtue pure and bright as well.

2. *Renewing the people* means causing all the people to know the proper path and to understand principle.

3. *Resting in the highest excellence* means that all people abide in the most excellent place.

What are the eight articles? They are investigating things, extending knowledge, rectifying the mind, making the

何謂八條目？就是「格物，致知，正心，誠意，修身，齊家，治國，平天下。」

（一）格物：研究天地間萬事萬物之性理。

（二）致知：運用智慧仔細分析物理，知道究竟。

（三）正心：端正一身所主宰的心。

（四）誠意：誠實所發之意。

（五）修身：修好自己的身（德行）。

這五種是屬於身心之學。

（六）齊家：整齊自己的家。

（七）治國：治理自己的國家。

（八）平天下：令天下太平。

這三種是屬於政治之學。

這是孔子之學說，是最基本之理想，也是儒教所依據之道理。今將《大學》中的三綱領和八條目略釋，將來再詳細的解釋。

intent sincere, cultivating oneself, regulating the family, managing the state, and bringing peace to the world.

1. *Investigating things* means investigating the natures and principles of the myriad things of the universe.

2. *Extending knowledge* means using one's wisdom to analyze in detail the principles of all phenomena, so that ultimate knowledge can be attained.

3. *Rectifying the mind* means making one's mind, which is the master of the body, proper and upright.

4. *Making the intent sincere* means being sincere in one's thinking.

5. *Cultivating oneself* means cultivating one's own virtuous conduct.

These five articles pertain to the study of body and mind.

6. *Regulating the family* means managing one's own family.

7. *Managing the state* means governing one's country well.

8. *Bringing peace to the world* means causing tranquility to prevail throughout the entire world.

These last three articles pertain to the study of politics.

These are the fundamental ideas of Confucius' teaching, and also the principles upon which Confucianism is based. Today I have briefly explained the three guidelines and the eight articles. A more detailed explanation may be given in the future.

禮運大同篇

首先要背熟，深而思之，
篤而行之。

大道之行也，天下爲公。

選賢與能，講信修睦。

故人不獨親其親，不獨子其子。

使老有所終，壯有所用，幼有所長。

矜寡孤獨廢疾者，皆有所養。

男有分，女有歸。

貨惡其棄於地也，不必藏於己。

力惡其不出於身也，不必爲己。

是故謀閉而不興，盜竊亂賊而不作。

故外戶而不閉。是謂大同。

Achieving Universal Harmony through the Use of Propriety

First memorize it by heart, then deeply ponder it, and finally put it into practice.

"When the Great Way prevails, every person is a part of society, and society belongs to everyone. The virtuous and the able are chosen for public office. Trustworthiness and friendliness are valued by all. People not only love their own parents and children, but love the parents and children of others as well. The elderly live their last years in happiness; able-bodied adults are usefully employed; children are reared properly. Widowers, widows, orphans, the childless aged, the handicapped and the ailing are well cared for. All men share their social responsibilities, and all women have their respective roles. Natural resources and commodities are not wasted or appropriated for selfish ends. People want to contribute their strength and ability to the society for public good, not for private gain. Deception and cheating cannot occur in such a society. Robbery, larceny, rebellions, and other crimes all disappear. Gates and doors are not locked; no one even thinks of stealing. This is a world where harmony, equality, and justice prevail."

這《禮運大同篇》描述孔子的理想世界。能成就大同世界，天下就太平。沒有戰爭，人人和睦相處，豐衣足食，安居樂業。這是孔子的政治政策，可惜行不通，因為人人皆自私自利的緣故。

「禮運」：大家皆在「禮」的道路上走，「運」行不息。人人知道明禮，從不明白處載運到明白處。

「大同」：整個世界都是一家人，人人愛彼如己。沒有欺騙的行為，以誠相待，互相援助。大同，就是世界和平的藍圖，所以孫逸仙先生將此篇從《禮記》中提出來，極力提倡「天下為公」。簡單地說，大同乃是你我一樣，沒有彼此、人我、是非之分別。人人自由，人人平等，就是極樂世界。

「大道之行也」：大道，就是共同遵守，而去行持的一個法則。這個光明大道，你也可以走，我也可以走，並非私人的道路。你修，則是你的大道光明

This "Essay on the Achievement of Universal Harmony, Equality, and Justice through the Use of Propriety" describes the ideal society of Confucius. If this world of harmony, equality, and justice is realized, peace will prevail under Heaven. Wars will disappear, and everyone will be friendly toward each other. People will be well fed and clothed, live peacefully, and be content with their occupations. That was Confucius' political strategy. Unfortunately, it could not be carried out because people were all selfish and concerned with personal gain.

Through the Use of Propriety: Everyone walks on the path of propriety, and the uses of propriety never cease. People understand propriety. They are brought to this understanding by observing the functioning of propriety.

Universal Harmony, Equality, and Justice: The whole world becomes one family. People love each other just as they love themselves. Cheating does not happen. People treat each other with sincerity and aid each other in times of need. Such universal harmony, equality, and justice is the blueprint for world peace. That was why Dr. Sun Zhongshan (Sun Yatsen) took this passage from the *Book of Rites* and advocated its ideal that "every person is a part of society, and society belongs to everyone." In short, universal harmony, equality, and justice means that you and I are the same; there is no distinction of you and me, me and others, right and wrong. Everyone is free, and everyone is equal. This is the world of ultimate bliss.

When the Great Way prevails: The Great Way is the law that everyone upholds and abides by. This great, bright way is

；我修，則是我的大道光明。這條光明平坦的大道，直接通達大同世界。

「天下爲公」：人人不爭、不貪、不求、不自私、不自利、不妄語，自然大公無私。若能達到這種程度，那就是天下爲公。這是孔子所提倡的民主政治，因他願恢復堯舜「禪讓」的政治。

「選賢與能」：選舉國家元首時，要選賢而有德者，要選有才幹，有智慧，有辦事能力的人，這種人能爲人類謀幸福，能爲國家圖富強。

「講信修睦」：對於鄰國講信用，互相不欺騙，和睦相處。言顧行，行顧言，沒有欺詐行爲。人與人之間要和睦，家與家之間要和睦，國與國之間要和睦。大家講道義，不講利害，自然無戰爭。

「故人不獨親其親」：因爲這樣大公無私的緣故，所以人人相親相愛。不但孝順自己的父母，也要孝順他人的父母，所謂「老吾老，以及人之老」，以

not a private path; you can walk on it and so can I. You cultivate your own great, bright way, and I cultivate my own. This broad, bright, and smooth path leads straight to the world of universal harmony, equality, and justice.

Every person is a part of society, and society belongs to everyone: If people don't fight, seek, pursue personal advantage, or lie, and aren't selfish or greedy, then naturally they will become just and impartial. In that case, every person will be a part of the society which belongs to everyone. That was the kind of democracy advocated by Confucius. He wanted to restore the policy of giving the throne to the able, which had been practiced by Emperors Yao and Shun.

The virtuous and the able are chosen for public office: When we choose the leaders for our country, we must choose people with virtue, ability, wisdom, and caliber. That kind of people will seek happiness for living beings and work to make the country affluent and strong.

Trustworthiness and friendliness are valued by all: This means dealing with neighboring countries in a trustworthy manner, getting along in a friendly way, and not cheating each other. Our conduct is consistent with our words. There is no trickery. There is harmony among people, among families, and among countries. Everyone is concerned with justice, not with advantages and disadvantages. At that point there naturally won't be any wars.

People not only love their own parents and children but love parents and children of others as well: Because there is no partiality, people can all treat one another with care and

事奉自己父母的心，照樣去事奉他人的父母，令他人的父母也得到快樂。

「不獨子其子」：不單獨慈愛自己的子女，也要慈愛他人的子女，所謂「幼吾幼，以及人之幼。」以教育自己子女的心，照樣去教育他人的子女，令他人的子女也得到學識。

「使老有所終」：設備完善的安老院，好好照顧老年人，令他們快樂，享受天年。無掛無礙，無煩無惱，無疾而終，往生西方極樂世界。

「壯有所用」：年輕力壯的人，一定要在社會服務，盡其所能，貢獻於國家。不可領失業救濟金，或福利金，否則成為國家的大包袱。應該努力工作，維持社會的秩序，不可遊手好閒，殃及國家。

「幼有所長」：年幼的兒童，必須好好教育他們，如何孝順父母，如何忠於國家，如何忠於職守。在這種教育長大，將來一定是優良的公民。

affection. Be filial not only to your own parents, but to the parents of others as well. It is said, "Care for your own elders and extend the same care to the elders of others." Take the same heart that you have when serving your own parents to serve the parents of others, and make them happy as well.

Love not only your own children, but the children of others as well. It is said, "Look after your own children and extend the same concern to the children of others." Take the heart that you have when educating your own youngsters to educate the youth of others, and cause them to acquire knowledge as well.

The elderly live their last years in happiness: There are nursing homes with good facilities to take care of the elderly and make them happy. That way the old people will be able to enjoy their last years without impediments, worries, or afflictions. As a result, they will die a natural death and get reborn in the Western Land of Ultimate Bliss.

Able-bodied adults are usefully employed: Young people with strong bodies must work and serve the society, and do their best to contribute to their country. They should not live on social welfare or unemployment benefits, because those cause them to become a great burden to society. People should work hard and maintain order in society, and not idly hang around causing trouble within the country.

Children are reared properly: Young children should be taught how to be filial to their parents, how to be loyal to their

「矜寡孤獨廢疾者」：「矜」，是憐愍、愛護、同情的意思。老而無妻為「鰥」，老而無夫為「寡」，幼年喪父母為「孤」，老年喪子女為「獨」，有殘廢的人為「廢」，有疾病的人為「疾」，這六種情形是世上最痛苦的人。

「皆有所養」：令這些不幸的人，生活得到安定，精神沒有威脅，生命有保障，國家設立種種機構，收養他們，治療他們。

「男有分」：男人有男人的本分、地位、責任，為國為家，要盡應盡的義務。不可好吃懶做，成為不良份子。

「女有歸」：婦女有所歸宿。相夫教子，做個賢妻良母，這就是女人的責任。各人安居於己之崗位，不錯位、不濫權，不可男女互相爭權，男主外，女主內。各有所主，各有所守。

country, and how to fulfill their duties faithfully. Children growing up with that kind of education will surely be fine citizens in the future.

Widowers, widows, orphans, the childless aged, the handicapped and the ailing are well cared for: Be kind and compassionate toward, love and protect, and sympathize with widowers, old people who have no wives; widows, old people who have no husbands; orphans; childless seniors; the handicapped; and the ailing, people with sickness. Those six kinds of people are the most unfortunate ones in the world. They should live a secure and peaceful life that is free of any threats to their psychological wellbeing. Their lives should be protected. The government should set up various institutions to take them in and provide them with proper care.

All men share their social responsibilities: Men have their duties, positions, and responsibilities. They should fulfill their obligations to their families and their country. They cannot be lazy or become deadbeats.

All women have their respective roles: All women have families. They should assist their husbands, teach their children, and be able wives and good mothers. Those are the duties of women. Everyone is content with his or her position and role, and doesn't try to change it or abuse his or her rights. Men are in charge of external affairs and women of domestic affairs. Men and women shouldn't fight with each other for their rights. They should each have their respective responsibilities and rights.

中國主張男女有別，爲避嫌疑，男女不交談，所謂

　　　　瓜田不納履，李下不正冠。

爲維持禮教，男女保持距離，所謂

　　　　叔嫂不授受，長幼不並肩。

「貨惡其棄於地也」：「貨」指一切糧食和一切物資，「惡」是不願意的意思，「棄」是糟蹋、浪費、損失。不可以將糧食糟蹋，不可以將物資浪費。好像現在糧食過剩的國家，不可以抛到大海中，不可用火焚掉，那是暴殄天物，將來必受報應。

「不必藏於己」：有物資要互相交換，不必藏私，認爲奇貨可居，以待善價。更不可操縱把持，應該以貨易貨，公平交易，這個國家沒有，那個國家有，可以交換。利己利人，何樂而不爲！如果不肯這樣做，那就是「貨棄於地藏於己」的行爲。

「力惡其不出於身也」：力是能力，所學的本領技能，不是自己專用，而是要爲世界人類服務，所謂

The Chinese prefer men and women be separated. In order to avoid suspicion, men and women do not chat with each other. It is said, "Never bend down and put on your shoes in the middle of a melon patch; never get up and touch your hat while standing underneath a plum tree." In order to maintain propriety, men and women should keep some distance between each other. It is said, "A brother and a sister-in-law do not give things to or receive things from each other; adults and children do not walk side by side."

Natural resources and commodities are not wasted: Natural resources and commodities refer to all kinds of food and commodities. We should not squander food or waste commodities. Countries with a surplus of agricultural produce should not dump the excess in the ocean or burn it up. That would be wasting natural resources, and it would surely bring on a retribution in the future.

Or appropriated for selfish ends: Commodities should be circulated, not hidden for selfish ends, hoarded for higher prices, or monopolized. There should be fair trading of commodities. One country should exchange its surplus goods with other countries to get the things it lacks. That is benefiting both self and others. Isn't that a positive thing to do? If we refuse to trade, it is the same as wasting goods or appropriating them for selfish ends.

People want to contribute their strength and ability to the society for public good: The knowledge and skills we have learned are not for our own use. Instead, they should be used to serve the people of the world. That is called "learning in order to put to good use."

「不必爲己」：不爲己謀。無論何事，不爲自己打算，而爲眾生著想。要有「捨己爲人」的精神，這是做人起碼的道理。

「是故」：因爲這種種的緣故，所以大家坦白率直，在世界上沒有勾心鬥角的思想，沒有明爭暗奪的行爲。

「謀閉而不興」：謀是計謀，關是關閉。計謀沒有了，把爭奪欺騙的門關上了，不會有「掛羊頭賣狗肉」的手段騙錢，這種不正當的行爲，也不會興起了。

「盜竊亂賊而不作」：明搶爲「盜」，暗偷爲「竊」，「亂賊」是造反的人。因爲不公平，你有他沒有，才發生盜竊事件。如果人人生活安定，豐衣足食，盜竊自然消失。人民皆因飢荒而搞革命，弄得民不聊生，十室九空，流離失所，苦不堪言，所謂「勝者王侯，敗者賊」，也就是亂賊。如果人人有工作，人人有飯吃，亂賊自然消滅。

Not for private gain: Never scheme for yourself. No matter what, you should make plans not just for yourself, but for all living beings. We must have this spirit of devoting ourselves to others; that is a basic principle of being a person.

Because of the reasons given above, people are frank with each other and do not scheme or fight against each other either openly or covertly.

Deception and cheating cannot occur in such a society: There is no more deception. The door of fighting and cheating is closed. Dishonest tactics to cheat people of their money are not used. Such improper conduct no longer prevails.

Robbery, larceny, rebellion, and other crimes all disappear: To take something by force is robbery; to steal it covertly is larceny; uprising against the government is rebellion. When there is unfairness, such as one person having things another one doesn't have, robbery and larceny will occur. If everyone lives a secure and peaceful life with adequate food and clothing, robbery and larceny will naturally disappear. People revolt when there are famines and they don't have enough to eat. When it is impossible to make a living, nine out of ten houses are deserted, their occupants becoming homeless wanderers. Such misery is unspeakable. It is said, "The winner becomes the king, and the losers become bandits," or rebels. If everyone is employed and well fed, rebels will naturally disappear.

「故外戶而不閉」：到了這種境界，沒有内憂，沒有外患，人人奉公守法。那時，路不拾遺，夜不閉戶，風調雨順，國泰民安。

「是謂大同」：這就是大同世界。人人不自私、不自利。人人公平，人人和樂，天下太平。

（編按：此篇乃萬佛聖城各階層學校的必修課。無論育良小學、培德中學、法界佛教大學的學生，首先要背熟，深而思之，篤而行之，此爲本會辦義務教育，重整道德扭轉頹風，正化民心的基礎，來成就將來的大同世界。）

一九八三年九月二十八日

Gates and doors are not locked: In this state of affairs, there are no internal troubles and no external calamities. Everyone abides by the law. At that time no one will take things found in the street that other people have lost. Since no one even thinks of stealing, doors and gates are not locked at night. The weather becomes temperate and the whole country becomes safe and peaceful.

This is a world where harmony, equality, and justice prevail. No one is selfish or pursues personal advantage. Everyone is honest, just, happy, and friendly, and so the world is peaceful.

[Editor's note: This essay of the *Book of Rites* is required course material in all the schools at the City of Ten Thousand Buddhas. All students of Instilling Goodness Elementary School, Developing Virtue Secondary School, and Dharma Realm Buddhist University must first memorize it, then deeply ponder it, and finally put it into practice. This is the basis upon which Dharma Realm Buddhist Association establishes its free education, reformation of social morals, reversal of the decadent trends of society, and rectifying of people's minds, in order to achieve a world of harmony, equality, and justice in the future.]

A talk given on September 28, 1983

如何做一個
有為的青年人

大家若能尊師重道，
力求上進，則前途無可限量。

各位同學！今天與你們見面，我心裏很高興。你們都是有爲的青年人，可是，有爲的學生要做「有爲」的事，若是頹靡不振，不能尊師重道，敦品立德，發憤讀書，那麼，就算「有爲」也變成「無爲」了！反過來說，大家若能尊師重道，力求上進，則前途無可限量，來日可作每個家庭的好榜樣，每個國家的領袖，全世界的主人翁。

你們想成爲家庭的好榜樣、國家的領袖、世界的主人翁嗎？現在教你們一個好辦法：第一，在家必要孝順父母，父母叫你，要趕快回答，不可慢條斯理

How to Be a Young Person of Achievement

If you can respect the teachers and the Way, and strive to progress in your studies, then you will have a promising future.

Fellow students, I am very glad to meet all of you today. You are all young people of achievement. However, in order to be a person of achievement you must have some achievement. If you are indolent, disrespectful to your teachers and the Way, and fail to create virtue and study hard, then your achievement is no achievement at all. On the other hand, if you can respect your teachers and the Way, and strive to progress in your studies, you will have a promising future. Then you can set a good example for all families and become leaders of nations and influential people in the world.

Do you want to set a good example for all families and become leaders of nations and of the world? Now let me tell you how to do it: First of all you must be filial to your parents at home. When they call you, you should respond

。父母叫你做事，你不可存不滿心，苟且懶惰。父母教訓你，叫你好好讀書，你就應該先把功課做好，才出去玩。不要蹦蹦跳跳，終日只看電視而忽略功課。你有什麼不對，父母懲罰你，你也應該順從接受。身爲子女，身爲學生，這種行爲最低限度能做到。做人的基礎，是在每個家庭裏建立起來的。

第二，要將以上孝順父母之精神，轉到學校裏來，恭敬老師。不要面從心違、陽奉陰違。考試時更不可作弊來欺騙老師。要做忠實的學生，長大後忠於國家。切不可生輕慢師長的心！老師們費盡心血來栽培你們這些小苗，令你們苗壯長大，本固枝榮，前途無量。切不可鬥爭老師、欺負師長。

現在社會的風氣壞到極點，甚至因些小學、中學及大學生，鬥爭老師。這種狂妄之行爲，欺師滅祖，不如禽獸。你們既然到了金輪聖寺，在這兒念書，必定是有大善根，才得到這麼好的老師來敎導你們。你們要珍惜這個機會，不要浪費寶貴光陰。

immediately and not take your time answering. When they ask you to do something, you shouldn't be upset or lazy. When they admonish you and tell you to study hard, you should finish doing your homework before you go out to play. Don't just goof off or spend the whole day watching television, neglecting your school work. When you do something wrong, you should accept their punishment obediently. As a child and a student, that is the very least that you should do. A person's moral foundation is developed within the family.

Next, you should bring this spirit of filiality to school and be respectful to your teachers. Do not feign compliance. Do not cheat on tests. Be an honest student now and a loyal citizen when you grow up. Never look down on your teachers. They use all their energy to cultivate you young shoots, to make you thrive and grow, to make your trunk strong and branches thick so that your future will be promising. You should never fight with or bully your teacher.

The demoralization of society is now very extreme. Some elementary, secondary, and college students are already fighting their teachers. Such unscrupulous conduct is worse than that of animals. You all must have wholesome roots that enable you to come to this monastery and have such good teachers instruct you. You should cherish this opportunity and not waste precious time.

切記！將來的目標，是要幫助社會，不是為自己發財做大官。首先要把道德的基礎打好。古時的人讀書為了「明理」，現在的人讀書多為「名利」。明理，就是研究如何治理國家，如何影響世界，移風易俗，做一些真實而有價值的事業。不是只顧自己生活能有多少享受。或想：「我將來做個醫生，賺更多的錢！」這種為名為利的思想太狹窄，太沒出息！

你若把道德基礎打好了，名利是小問題。將來堪為世界的主人翁，能做一番偉大的事業。現在是你們的黃金時代，不要錯過，否則將來後悔莫及。我這一番話是苦口婆心對你們說，所謂：

> 忠言逆耳利於行，
> 良藥苦口利於病。

不管你愛不愛聽，我是盡了我一番心意！

一九八三年十一月
開示於美國加州洛杉磯金輪聖寺

Remember that your future goal is to help society, not to make money or get a high position. First of all, you should build a good foundation of virtue. The ancients studied for the purpose of understanding principles. Nowadays people study for the purpose of obtaining fame and benefit. Understanding principles involves studying how to govern a country, how to influence the world to change its unwholesome customs and habits, and how to carry out genuine and worthwhile endeavors. In life, you shouldn't be concerned with just your own enjoyment. You shouldn't think: "I want to be a physician, because they make a lot of money!" Such thoughts of fame and profit are petty and useless.

If you establish a good foundation of virtue, then fame and benefit are hardly an issue. You'll be influential people who will achieve great things in the world. Now is your golden age. Don't let it pass by in vain, or you will regret it later. It is said,

> Truthful words jar the ear,
> But help one to act wisely.
> Good medicine is bitter to the taste,
> But cures the sickness.

Whether or not you care to listen, I have tried my best.

A talk given on November 1983,
at Gold Wheel Sagely Monastery, Los Angeles

不幸之中的幸運人

樹若是沒有根，或者露到泥土上，
這個樹就會倒塌。

我們生長在一個不幸的時代。世間上的誘惑力太厲害了，令人紙醉金迷，利令智昏。日新月異的科學發明，令人把「根本」都忘了。在這個不幸的時代中，若是能認識環境而不隨波逐流，不同流合污，就能改變你的命運，做一個幸運的人。

我們人的根本是什麼呢？孔子說：「君子務本，本立而道生。孝悌也者，其為仁之本歟。」人的根本就是「孝悌」兩個字。在西方，人人都忘本了，根本就不知道什麼是「孝悌」；這就好像把樹木的根

Fortunate People in Unfortunate Times

If a tree has no roots, or the roots are exposed, then the tree will fall.

We live in an unfortunate time. The temptations of this world are too powerful and make people indulge in a wanton life. Profits dim their wisdom. Rapid scientific development has caused people to forget their foundation. During this unfortunate time, if we can recognize the situation and not go along with it, we'll be able to change our destiny and become fortunate people.

What is the basis for being a person? Confucius said, "A superior person devotes himself to the foundation. When the foundation is established, the Way will come forth. Filiality and fraternal respect are the basis of humaneness." So the basis of a person is "filiality and fraternal respect." But in the West people neglect this foundation. They don't

刨出來一樣——樹若是沒有根，或者露到泥土上，這個樹就會倒塌。人要是不懂得「孝」義，也等於樹木沒紮下根一樣，如何成一個有用的人呢？

君子要務本。在家要孝順父母，悌敬兄長。要幫助家裏的操作，不可好吃懶作。若能找到根本，那麼，就在這個世運不安、不幸的時代裏，能做一個卓然獨立，出類拔萃的幸運人。小朋友！你們應該做

疾風中之勁燭，

烈火裏的精金。

風愈大，這根蠟燭愈燒得光亮。人人顛倒發狂，而你不受物欲所誘惑，不同流合污，這就像疾風中之勁燭，真金是不怕火煉。你如何燒它，其份量不減，因爲這個金是純真的。你們要像真金，任何烈火也燒不壞。

一九八三年十一月開示洛杉磯金輪聖寺

even know what filiality and fraternal respect are. This is just like digging out the roots of a tree. If a tree has no roots, or the roots are exposed, then the tree will fall. People who don't understand filiality and fraternal respect are just like trees without roots. How can they be useful?

A superior person devotes himself to the foundation. At home you should be filial to your parents and respectful towards your siblings, help with the housework, and not be a lazy glutton. If you pay attention to the basics, you can become an outstanding and fortunate person in this turbulent time. Young friends, make yourselves into

> Strong candles in the gusty wind;
> Pure gold in the blazing fire.

The gustier the wind, the brighter the candle burns. Other people may become mad and deluded, but you won't be tempted by material desires; you won't go along with the crowd. Be like a strong candle in the gusty wind. Pure gold is not afraid of being smelted in the blazing fire. No matter how you smelt it, it will not lessen, because it is pure. You should be like pure gold that cannot be harmed by any fire.

A talk given on November, 1983,
at the Gold Wheel Sagely Monastery, Los Angeles

行住坐臥有威儀

四大威儀，
是日常生活中要注意的儀態。

小朋友！你們應該像蓮花，蓮花又美，又香潔，人見人愛。它是出淤泥而不染，沒有塵埃，不俗氣，所以殊貴。在這個人人瘋狂、人人顛倒的時代，你若能找到根本，而不去同流合污，也就像蓮花那麼高貴。

你們將來都有機會成為社會國家的棟樑，但先要把枝椏剪去，也就是將不良的習氣毛病盡除，這才能成為棟樑之材。若是不雕琢自己，這就和一般俗人一樣，這個世界也不會進步。所以，欲想改良這個

Walking, Standing, Sitting and Reclining with Dignity

We should pay attention to the Four Modes of Deportment in our daily lives.

Young friends, you should be like lotus blossoms: beautiful, pure, and fragrant. Everyone likes them. The lotus flower grows out of the mud, but is not stained by the mud. It isn't defiled or common; on the contrary, it is rare and precious. In times like this, when people are mad and confused, if you can discover your roots and not be swept along by the crowd, you'll be as noble and precious as a lotus flower.

You all have the opportunity to become supporting pillars of society and the nation. But first you have to prune the branches, that is, do away with all improper habits, so that you can become a useful person. If you don't refine yourself, you'll be just like ordinary people, and the world will never improve that way. If you want to reform the world and change its negative trends, you have to set

世界，移風易俗，必要在年輕時代就立下宗旨，並且，還要有「陪襯」，來幫助你向前發展。

什麼是「陪襯」呢？就是「行住坐臥」四大威儀，都有一定的法則，不可雜亂無章。好像很多學生，走路的時候不是走路，他是蹦蹦跳跳，東張西望，像猴子一樣，這就完全沒有威儀啦！所謂「行如風，坐如鐘，臥如弓，立如松」。

「行如風」：走路時，有如「輕風徐來，水波不興。」這個風是輕風，不是暴風、龍捲風，起屋拔樹，大家要注意！

「坐如鐘」：坐的時候，要像大鐘那麼穩固，但不要像鐘擺，搖來搖去，要坐得很端正，尤其是女孩子，不要把腳晃來晃去。

「臥如弓」：躺著的時候像一把弓，也有一定的姿態。

「立如松」：站著的時候，如一棵大松樹，又高又直，卓然獨立，不是像蛇那樣子，彎彎曲曲。

guidelines for yourselves when you are young. You will also need support to help you advance along the way.

What provides this support? The Four Modes of Deportment: walking, standing, sitting and reclining. There are set rules for all of these; we cannot go about them in a sloppy manner. Many students don't walk properly; they bounce and leap, peering east and west like monkeys. That shows a lack of deportment. It is said, "Walk like the breeze, sit like a bell, recline like a bow, and stand like a pine."

"Walk like the breeze": When we walk, we should be like "a soft breeze that makes no ripples on the water." This wind is a soft breeze, not a storm or a whirlwind that blows down houses and uproots trees. We should be careful about this.

"Sit like a bell": When we sit, we should be as steady as a big bell. Don't be like the bell clapper, swinging to and fro. You should sit upright and not swing your legs, especially if you are a girl.

"Recline like a bow": When we lie down, our bodies should look like bows; this is the posture for reclining.

"Stand like a pine": When we stand, we should look like great pine trees, tall and straight, singularly outstanding. We shouldn't be bent and curved like snakes.

四大威儀，是日常生活中要注意的儀態。就在學生時代，應該把這些基本學會了。凡事「擇善而從，不善而改。」「是道則進，非道則退。」我對你們所說的話，是破斧沉舟，至誠懇切。希望你們好自為之，否則，莫如行屍走肉，酒囊飯袋，對這個世界毫無貢獻！

We should pay attention to the Four Modes of Deportments in our daily lives and learn these basic things when we are students. We should always choose to follow good examples and change conduct that is not virtuous. "If it's the Way, advance upon it; if it's not the Way, retreat from it." I tell you all this in utmost sincerity. I hope you will put forth your best effort. Otherwise you will simply be bodies that can walk around and consume food and drink, but that make no contributions to the world.

讀書簡單之祕訣

有種種不好的動作，
心裏就昏亂，讀什麼書也記不下。

小朋友！你們坐在那兒，手又動，腳又搖，頭又晃
，要把頭搬到腳那裏去，又要把腳搬到頭上，這就
是顛倒。有這種種不好的動作，心裏就昏亂，讀什
麼書也記不下。應該端然正坐，頭腦冷靜，對老師
所講的任何課，特別留神，這樣才能吸收知識。
讀書有很簡單的方法，就是「三上、三到」。

「三上」：路上、枕上、廁上。在路上走，一邊在
想：「今天老師教我什麼課呢？那個字怎麼寫？那
句話什麼意義？」在路上走時，要不停地思惟剛學

The Simple Secret to Studying

When you are moving around, your mind will be confused and muddled.

Young friends, you are sitting there, moving your hands, swinging your legs, shaking your heads, wanting to move your heads to where your legs are, then again wanting to move your legs to where the head is. That is being upside-down. When you are moving around like that, your mind is confused and muddled. Then you won't be able to memorize what you have studied. You should sit upright with a clear head and concentrate on the teacher's lecture. That way you'll be able to absorb knowledge.

There is a very simple method of study that involves three places and three faculties. The three places for studying are: on the road, on the pillow and on the toilet. When you're walking down the road, you can think to yourself: "What did the teacher teach today? How is that word written?

習的功課。回到家裏，每天晚間躺到床上，還沒有睡著之前，應該把當天所學的課重新默念一遍，這時候你的腦海裏沒有那麼多雜念，應該很容易記得。在廁上，也不要浪費時間打妄想，還是在心裏研究課本。

「三到」：眼到、口到、心到。用眼看書，用口讀誦，用心思惟研究。這三到缺一不可。要用冷靜的頭腦分析所學到的道理，才不至辜負老師們的心血和時間。記住！你們努力讀書，長大後要利益社會，造福人類！

What is the meaning of this sentence?" Walking along, you contemplate what you have just learned at school. Back home, every night before you fall asleep, you should also mentally review what you have learned that day. At that moment, your mind doesn't have too many random thoughts, so you should be able to memorize things easily. When you go to the toilet, you shouldn't waste time daydreaming, but should instead review your lessons.

The three faculties you use in studying are: the eyes, the mouth, and the mind. You use your eyes to read, your mouth to recite, and your mind to contemplate. You cannot overlook any one of these three faculties. Analyze the principles you have learned with a clear head, so you won't disappoint the teachers after all the time and effort they have expended in teaching you. Remember to study hard, contribute to society when you grow up, and benefit all of humanity.

萬佛聖城七週年紀念

萬佛聖城有今日的成就，
乃是佛教徒經千辛萬苦奮鬥得來之成果。

（一）佛法光臨全世界

萬佛聖城成立已經七年，聖城有今日的成就，乃是佛教徒經千辛萬苦奮鬥得來之成果。其間不可思議的事蹟，不勝枚舉！眼見聖城目前一片蓬勃的生機，應從頭說起：

二十餘年前，宣化老和尚觀察機緣成熟，乃毅然隻身來美，把正法種子，散播在西半球肥沃的土地上。多年來勤奮開墾，含辛茹苦，豎正法幢，轉大法輪。

The Seventh Anniversary of the City of Ten Thousand Buddhas

The present accomplishments of the City of Ten Thousand Buddhas result from the toil and efforts of Buddhist disciples in overcoming numerous hardships.

I. The Buddha's Teachings Spread Worldwide

The City of Ten Thousand Buddhas has been in existence for seven years now. Its present accomplishments result from the toil and efforts of Buddhist disciples in overcoming numerous hardships. Countless miracles have occurred. Let us recount from the beginning how this flourishing City started.

Over twenty years ago, the Venerable Master Hsuan Hua saw that the conditions were ripe and traveled alone to America to sow the seeds of Proper Dharma in the fertile soil of the Western Hemisphere. Through the years he has arduously blazed new trails, enduring hardship in order to raise the banner of the Proper Dharma and turn the great wheel of Dharma.

一九六二年抵美時，在三藩市華埠成立「佛教講堂」，自號「墓中僧」，韜光晦跡。一九六八年爲西雅圖大學生們開講《楞嚴經》，成立「中美佛教總會」（法界佛教總會的前身）。隨後，其他隸屬本會之機構，如「金山聖寺」（一九七〇年）、「國際譯經學院」（一九七二年）、洛杉磯市「金輪聖寺」（一九七五年），曼第仙奴縣深谷，達摩鎮「萬佛聖城」（一九七六年）、西雅圖「達摩中心」（一九七六年）等正法道場，皆如雨後春筍，欣欣向榮，蓬勃發展，爲未來佛教奠定穩固的基礎。

（二）義務教育，重整社會頹風

上人化人宗旨，是以出世的精神，作入世的事業。有鑑於舉世道德頹靡，斯文掃地，師資不良，皆因教育失敗。家長不關心兒童前途，任其發展，學校訓導無方，不但不灌輸道德思想，反而鼓勵青少年盡做違背良心、傷天害理之行爲，難怪形成社會裏成千上萬的流氓太保，殺人放火，販毒奸賊，無惡不作。

Upon arriving in the United States in 1962, he founded the Buddhist Lecture Hall in San Francisco's Chinatown. He named himself "The Monk in the Grave" and lived in quiet anonymity. In 1968, the Master explained the *Shurangama Sutra* for students from the University of Washington in Seattle and founded the Dharma Realm Buddhist Association. In the years that followed, he founded various branches of the Dharma Realm Buddhist Association, including Gold Mountain Monastery (1970), the International Institute for the Translation of Buddhist Texts (1972), Gold Wheel Monastery in Los Angeles (1975), the City of Ten Thousand Buddhas in Talmage, Mendocino County (1976), Bodhidharma Center in Seattle (1976), and others. Like bamboo shoots after a spring rain, these Way-places of Proper Dharma thrived and prospered, laying a stable foundation for Buddhism's future.

II. Promoting Free Education to Reform Social Trends

In his transformation of people, the Venerable Master carries out worldly endeavors in a transcendental spirit. He sees the failure of education as the root cause for the decline of morals, the degradation of culture, and the poor quality of teaching. Parents allow children to do as they please, unconcerned for their futures. Schools are ineffective in educating and disciplining children. Instead of learning ethical values at school, children learn to ignore their consciences and violate natural principles. It's no wonder there are so many dropouts and juvenile delinquents who become involved in murder, arson, drug peddling, theft, and every conceivable crime.

上人純以德行感化叛逆青年，改邪歸正，甚至息滅幫派間之鬥爭，使社會安寧，默默幫助華人社會，厥功至偉！

上人一向熱心教育，少年時在東北已辦義學，蘊育精英。為拯救眼前教育淪亡之慘局，於一九八〇年美國國慶日宣佈，聖城所隸屬之學校，一律免收學費，而積極提倡「敦品立德」之軌範，以正化民心，移風易俗。自從一九七五年首創育良小學，繼而設立培德中學。小、中學是以男女分校上課，重禮節，講孝悌，諄諄善誘，使青年人從善如流。育良小學以「孝」為宗旨，培德中學以「忠孝」為宗旨，而法界佛教大學則以「忠孝仁義」為宗旨。

世界的命運，掌握在青年人手裏。苟不全心撫養栽培，後果不堪設想矣！故造就社會國家棟樑之材，為當務之急。本會所屬各階層之學府，旨在培育頂天立地、高風亮節的領袖人才，將來能廣被群生，則人類幸甚！

Purely by means of his virtue, the Venerable Master has influenced rebellious young people to reform. He has even ended gang wars, bringing peace to society. He has quietly helped the overseas Chinese, creating tremendous merit.

The Master has long been committed to education. As a teenager in Manchuria, he started a free school for poor children. Wishing to rescue education from its present predicament, the Master announced on the Fourth of July in 1980 that the schools at the City of Ten Thousand Buddhas would charge no tuition and would actively promote a model curriculum of ethical virtue and character so as to transform people's attitudes and reform social customs. Instilling Goodness Elementary was founded in 1975, followed by Developing Virtue Secondary School. In both schools, boys and girls study separately. Proper etiquette, filial piety, and fraternal respect are emphasized. Under skillful and patient instruction, young people behave virtuously as a matter of course. Instilling Goodness Elementary School focuses on the virtue of filial piety, while Developing Virtue Secondary School emphasizes service to society as well as filial piety. The aims of Dharma Realm Buddhist University are service, filial piety, humaneness, and justice.

The destiny of the world lies in the hands of young people. If we devote less than our full attention to their education, the consequences will be dire indeed! It is of critical importance to nurture young people who will be capable of leading and shaping society. The various educational institutions of this association aspire to foster outstanding future leaders of uncompromising integrity who will benefit all beings and bring blessings to humankind.

（三）人間福地，塵寰淨土

本會於一九七六年，購買萬佛聖城，七年來默默耕
耘，千魔不改，萬魔不退，受盡各方面的排斥與攻
擊；尤其佛教之獅蟲更加毀辱，唯恐天下不亂。然
聖城面對諸多橫逆，處之泰然，終於成爲享譽國際
的人間淨土，卓然獨立，耀人心目。聖城位於三藩
市以北一百一十五英里，面積爲四百餘英畝（包括
妙覺山在內）。四邊群山環抱，花草樹木，應有盡
有，如舉世知名的大紅木等。此外松柏翠竹，果樹
成行，相映成趣。城內有白鶴、孔雀、鸚鵡等，宣
演微妙法音。梅花鹿、松鼠及各種飛禽走獸，點綴
此人間聖境。城內巨型建築物七十餘棟，均以最高
級材料建築，可容納二萬住眾。城內空氣清新，瞻
仰朝觀者，置身其間，往往陶然忘機，頓入不思議
境界！

（四）國際道場，建設輝煌獨到

聖城不斷在籌建改良中，於一九八二年完成宏偉之
三拱山門，能兼作講臺之用。目前的「萬佛殿」，
除四壁萬佛莊嚴外，殿中則供奉高十八呎的千手千

III. A Pure Land of Blessings within the Mundane World

Since purchasing the City of Ten Thousand Buddhas in 1976, the association has quietly persevered in its work, undaunted by setbacks. The City has been discriminated against and attacked, being slandered by those who rely on Buddhism for their livelihood. Having calmly withstood all adversities, the City is now recognized as an international "pure land on earth". It stands strong, independent, and shining in its splendor.

The City is located 115 miles north of San Francisco and covers more than 400 acres of land, including Wonderful Enlightenment Mountain. Surrounded by mountains, the City has all kinds of trees, flowers, and vegetation, such as the world-famous redwood, pine, cedar, bamboo, and rows of fruit trees. White cranes, peacocks, and other birds sing the wondrous sounds of Dharma. Spotted deer, squirrels, and other wild creatures populate the grounds. Over seventy large buildings, constructed with materials of the best quality, house up to twenty thousand residents. Breathing the fresh, clean air and taking in the lovely setting, it is easy to fall into a reverie.

IV. An International Monastery of Imposing Architecture

The City has undertaken numerous construction and renovation projects. The magnificent triple-arch front gate, which doubles as a lecture platform, was completed in 1982. The walls of the Hall of Ten Thousand Buddhas are adorned with ten thousand small Buddha statues, and an eighteen-foot-tall statue of the Thousand-Handed,

眼觀世音菩薩聖像。此聖像靈驗事蹟，不勝枚舉，誠心禮拜者，每求必應，心想事成。故有世界各國人士絡繹不絕，接踵而至。

又於一九八二年完成「琉璃金剛寶戒壇」，壇內四壁寶鏡輝映，莊嚴宏偉歎未曾有。「五觀堂」於已成立，乃最新款之建設，能容納二千餘人同時用齋。城內有「如來寺」、大「慈悲院」（男眾）、大「喜捨院」（女眾），及馬鳴、龍樹、師子等各大精舍。此外還有針灸診所、綜合醫院（內有一百八十間病房）、難民救濟會、世界宗教中心等建設。

現正積極籌建大雄寶殿。該殿高一百一十餘呎，橫三百三十呎，縱二百一十呎，可容納萬人同時禮佛。樓下是華嚴正法大講堂，二樓爲大雄寶殿。外形雙疊飛簷，四面流水，磅礴壯觀，將爲西方規模最宏偉之佛殿。

蓋因美國爲國際間之大國，故佛教興起，必要有國際性水準之大型道場，始能將世界佛教領入燦爛輝煌之新階段！

Thousand-Eyed Guanshiyin Bodhisattva stands in the front of the hall. Countless miracles are associated with this statue of the Bodhisattva. Those who pray sincerely before it never fail to gain a response. Thus this statue is visited by an endless stream of pilgrims from every nation.

The Vajra Jeweled Ordination Hall, also completed in 1982, is unique in its magnificent design, which includes inter-reflecting mirrors on four walls. The Five Contemplations Dining Hall, the most recent project to be completed, has a seating capacity of two thousand. Dormitories in the City include Tathagata Monastery, Great Compassion House (for men), Joyous Giving House (for women), Horse Whinney House, Dragon Tree House, and Lion House. In addition, the City as an acupuncture clinic, a general hospital with 180 rooms for patients, the Buddhist Council for the Rescue and Resettlement of Refugees, and a Center for World Religions.

Funds are currently being raised to build a Jeweled Hall of Great Heroes that will be 110 feet high, 330 feet long, and 210 feet wide. It will hold up to ten thousand worshippers at once. The first floor will be the Flower Adornment Proper Dharma Lecture Hall, and the second floor will be the Jeweled Hall of Great Heroes. The structure will have double eaves with the corners curving upwards and be surrounded by flowing water. It will be colossal and magnificent, the most splendid Buddha Hall in the West.

Since the United States is a great nation of the world, we must have a large, international monastery to lead world Buddhism into its next stage of splendid achievements!

（五）六大宗旨，大公無私

萬佛聖城家風嚴峻，龍盤虎臥，緇素四眾，皆杜絕攀緣，不事媚俗，不同流合污。上人從出家以來，抱定六大宗旨：「不爭、不貪、不求、不自私、不自利、不妄語。」令其座下徒眾，皆養成磊落昂藏，志行高潔的道風。所謂

> 凍死不攀緣，
> 餓死不化緣，
> 窮死不求緣；
> 隨緣不變，不變隨緣，
> 抱定我們三大宗旨。
> 捨命爲佛事，
> 造命爲本事，
> 正命爲僧事；
> 即事明理，明理即事，
> 推行祖師一脈心傳。

乃是本會修行人之座右銘。儘量革除時下急功近利、投機取巧、貪圖捷徑、不肯吃虧之流弊，而腳踏

V. The Six Guiding Principles and Selfless Public Spirit

Under the high standards of integrity of the City of Ten Thousand Buddhas, the "dragons must coil up and the tigers must crouch down," so to speak. The members of the fourfold assembly avoid opportunism, flattery, and vulgar trends. As a monk, the Master has always lived by the Six Guidelines: not to fight, not to be greedy, not to seek, not to be selfish, not to pursue personal gain, and not to tell lies. As a result, his followers have developed uncompromising standards of integrity. The practitioners of our association take the following as their creed:

> Freezing, we do not scheme.
> Starving, we do not beg.
> Dying of poverty, we ask for nothing.
> According with conditions, we do not change.
> Not changing, we accord with conditions.
> We adhere firmly to our three great principles.
> We renounce our lives to do the Buddha's work.
> We take the responsibility to mold
>   our own destinies.
> We rectify our lives to fulfill the Sanghan's role.
> Encountering specific matters,
>   we understand the principles.
> Understanding the principles,
>   we apply them in specific matters.
> We carry on the single pulse of
> the Patriarchs' mind-transmission.

We try our best to avoid the utilitarian, opportunistic, and selfish attitudes common in this day and age. We strive to practice in an honest, down-to-earth fashion, devoting our

實地，真修實鍊，養成「大拙」精神，獻身佛教。上人教化眾生，全憑忍耐功夫，尤其是西方任性慣了難調難伏之青年人，無不被其德行感化以至心悅誠服。徒弟若不聽話，上人向彼叩頭。就是以此超人至誠懇切之忍耐力，來攝受眾生。

（六）世界佛教，放大光明

上人自來美二十餘年，無非本著「一日不作，一日不食」的大無畏精神，處處以身作則，誨人不倦。現時座下出家眾，包括華、美、義、越、馬等國籍，皆是思想卓越，學問淵深，精嚴戒律，唯以正法為樂，不拉攏白衣，不交際權貴，來者不拒，往者不追，不受私人供養，一切財產歸公家保管。如此振興宗風，重整毗尼，實行「公共道場」之高蹈懿行。

城中出家眾，依照佛制，日中一食，夜不倒單，抖擻精神，為使正法永住。四眾翻譯經典，廣辦教育，念佛參禪，禮懺持咒，無不專心向上，為法忘軀

lives to Buddhism with almost foolish sincerity. The Venerable Master uses nothing but patience to teach his disciples. Young Westerners in particular, who are used to listening to no one and having their own way, have been inspired to submit to him wholeheartedly. When his disciples fail to listen, the Master bows to them, using his superhuman sincerity and patience to gather in sentient beings.

VI. World Buddhism Shines Resplendently

Since coming to the United States over twenty years ago, the Venerable Master has consistently embodied the courageous spirit of the maxim: "I shall not eat on any day that I have done no work." He always teaches by example and does not know the meaning of fatigue when it comes to instructing people.

His monastic disciples, who are of Chinese, American, British, Vietnamese, and Malaysian origins, are characterized by their outstanding ideals, profound erudition, and strict moral discipline. They delight only in the Proper Dharma and do not exploit the laity or curry favors from the rich and powerful. Neither turning away those who come nor pursuing those who leave the monastery, these disciples turn all donations over to the temple and receive no personal offerings. In this way, they hope to reform Buddhism, revive the Vinaya (moral discipline), and practice the lofty and virtuous conduct of a public monastery.

The monastics at the City observe the Buddha's regulations of eating only one meal a day and not lying down to sleep. They practice vigorously so as to perpetuate the Proper Dharma. The fourfold assembly is engaged in translating

。然卻有佛教的癌病者，批評此非正法與中道，更譏爲標奇立異，眞不知彼等居心何在！

聖城鍾靈毓秀，人文蔚起，才智之士，代不乏人。在末法時代，灼破重昏，照明寰宇，助佛揚化，紹隆三寶。所謂

　　無不從此法界流，無不還歸此法界

此處乃是十方聖賢豪傑，薈萃之地也。今逢七週年慶祝大典，益加勇猛直前，誓與同仁，共入無量光明解脫境界！

the Buddhist canon, providing education through the schools, reciting the Buddha's name, meditating, practicing repentance, and reciting mantras. In all of these, they advance single-mindedly, forgetting themselves for the sake of the Dharma. Yet there are detractors in Buddhism who criticize such practices as not according with the Proper Dharma and the Middle Way, and who accuse us of showing off. It is hard to fathom their intentions.

In the City's auspicious environment, talented and learned individuals are not lacking. In this age of the Dharma's decline, they shine through the darkness to illuminate the universe, spreading the Buddha's teachings and perpetuating the Triple Jewel. It is said,

> There is nothing that does not flow forth
> from the Dharma Realm.
> There is nothing that does not return
> to the Dharma Realm.

This is the place where sages, worthies, and heroes of the ten directions convene. On this occasion of the City's Seventh Anniversary Celebration, may we advance with vigor and enter the realm of infinitely bright liberation together.

循規蹈矩勤耕耘

循規蹈矩，要依照規矩去做，
不要太放逸了，不要太浪漫了。
我對每一個人的期望都是這樣子。

光陰過得非常快，在不知不覺中暑假就過去了。在
中國，孔子說過人生就好像流水似地，川流不息；
時光過去就不會再回來了。又有人說：

> 一寸光陰一寸金，寸金難買寸光陰。

說這一寸的光陰，就好像一寸黃金那麼樣寶貴。可
是這黃金，你若丟了，還可以想法子再把它找回來
；這光陰過去了，就沒有法子再把它找回來了。由
這樣看來，這光陰比黃金更貴重。所以在佛教裏說
：「一寸時光就是一寸命光。」時光過去了，這個
命光也就少一點。所以才說：「時光減處命光微」

Abide by the Rules and Cultivate Diligently

We should certainly be people who abide by the rules and work according to the regulations. Don't be too lax or emotional. Those are my expectations for each one of you.

The time passes by very quickly. Without our realizing it, the summer is already over. In China, Confucius compared life to a ceaselessly flowing stream. Time that has gone by can never return. Someone also said,

> An inch of time is worth an inch of gold,
> but even if one has an inch of gold,
> one can hardly buy back an inch of time.

An inch of time is as valuable as an inch of gold. If you lose gold, it's possible to recover it. Once time has gone by, however, there is no way to get it back. Therefore, time is even more valuable than gold. Thus, in Buddhism we say, "An inch of time is an inch of life." When time grows short, one's life is also shorter. We must certainly value our time and not casually let it go by in vain.

，時光減少了，命光也就少一點了。我們對時間一定要看重了，不要把它隨隨便便地就放過去了。

我們這個暑假，由早晨六點鐘就開始，或者打坐，或者研究佛經。由早晨到晚間九點鐘這段時間，每一個人都很認真地去用功修行，我相信這個期間比黃金更貴重，比鑽石也更有價值。所以大家能以在一起聞熏聞修，在我們每個人生命裏頭，這段時間可以說是最寶貴，最有價值的一段時間。可惜這個時間不太長，轉眼之間就過去了；雖然過去了，可是我們每一個人所學的佛法，在每一個人的腦筋裏頭，在每一個人的八識田裏邊，都種下去一個寶貴的金剛種子。這個種子種下去了，等到將來一定會結金剛不壞的果；金剛不壞的果就是佛果，就是成佛。

那麼在什麼時候成呢？這就看我們每一個人自己的耕耘灌溉。這個種子種下去了，好像種田似地種到地裏頭，你必須要，譬如給它灌一點水，除一除草，把這個地耕得掀騰起來。怎麼樣叫除這個草呢？就是我們每一個人要時時刻刻防微杜漸。怎麼叫防

During this summer, we have begun our days at six o'clock in the morning, either meditating or studying the Buddhist Sutras. From early in the morning until nine o'clock at night, every person applies himself diligently to cultivation. I believe that this period has been more precious than gold, more valuable than diamonds. Everyone has been together, being permeated and influenced by what we have heard and cultivated.

This period of time could be considered a most precious and valuable time in each of our lives. It's a pity that this time is not that long; it has passed by in the twinkling of an eye. Although it is over, the Buddhadharma that each of us has learned has planted a precious *vajra* seed in our brain and in the field of our eight consciousness. This seed has been planted, and in the future it will certainly bear the indestructible fruit of *vajra*. The indestructible *vajra* fruit is also the Buddha-fruit; in other words, we will become Buddhas.

When will we become Buddhas? It depends on our own efforts at tilling and irrigating the fields. The seed has been planted in the ground, but, just as in farming, you have to water it, pull the weeds, and turn the soil by tilling it, making it soft so that the seed can sprout. How do you pull the weeds out? What does it mean to weed the ground? It means that at all times, each one of us must "guard against

微呢？防微就是防備，預防這個微細處；我們的心念不要打妄想，不要令它生很多雜念。杜漸就是杜絕，杜絕這一切的妄想，要把它沒有了。

每一天這樣地用功，每一天這樣去修行，栽培灌溉。就好像種田，我灌一點水，我再把地收拾得沒有草，那麼一天一天地你這個金剛種子種到地裏去，就生菩提的芽；菩提芽生出來將來就結菩提果。可是你要保護這個菩提芽，保護這個菩提果；你不要不管它了，也不灌水，也不去栽培它，那麼它就會枯槁了，會乾了。

你能以灌溉；怎麼叫灌溉呢？你就天天學習佛法，用佛法的法水來灌溉這個菩提芽，久而久之，你這個金剛的果也就會成就了。如果你過去了這個時間，不繼續地理它，這個金剛的種子種下去了是種下去了，它也不容易生出來的。你必須要好好地保護著你這個金剛的種子，不要再做以前所歡喜做的事情；就是要守規矩，循規蹈矩，不要再像以前那麼樣做一些個不守規矩的事情。你守規矩，這就合佛法；不守規矩就不合佛法。所以我們做人一定要循

what is subtle and stop what is gradually going to happen." That is, we must guard against the arising of very subtle thoughts. We must put a stop to all false thoughts, getting rid of them completely.

Every day we must apply effort in this way. Each day we must cultivate in this way, tending and irrigating the fields. It's just like farming. You give it some water and pull out all the weeds, day by day, and the *vajra* seed you have planted in the ground will produce a Bodhi sprout. After your Bodhi tree has produced shoots, that is, after your Bodhi sprout has come up, it will eventually bear the Bodhi fruit. But you have to protect that Bodhi sprout and Bodhi fruit. Don't neglect it. If you neglect to water it and tend to it, then it will wither away and dry up.

What is meant by watering? If you study the Buddhadharma every day and use the Dharma water of the Buddhadharma to irrigate your Bodhi sprout, then over the course of time, your *vajra* fruit will come to maturity. If you don't continue to care for this *vajra* seed after this period is over, then even though it was planted, it won't be easy for it to sprout. You must protect your *vajra* seed well. Don't go back to doing the things you used to like doing. Follow the rules and behave yourselves. Don't be as rowdy as you used to be. Don't do the heedless things that you used to do. If you follow the rules, then you are in accord with the Buddhadharma. If you don't follow the rules, then you are not in accord with the Buddhadharma. We should certainly

規蹈矩，要依照規矩去做去，不要太放逸了，不要太浪漫了。我對每一個人的期望都是這樣子。

在這個暑假的期間，講這部《楞嚴經》，這一定是所謂「一歷耳根，永爲道種。」經耳朵一聽，這個經典的道理就永遠在你八識田裏邊，有這種菩提的種子。

一九六八年九月於三藩市佛教講堂

講解《楞嚴經》時

be people who abide by the rules and work according to the regulations. Don't be too lax or overly emotional. Those are my expectations for each one of you.

During this summer session of lectures on the *Shurangama Sutra*, it has surely been the case that, "Once it enters your ears, it is forever a seed of the Way." As soon as the principles of this Sutra pass through your ears, they remain forever in the field of your eighth consciousness as seeds of Bodhi.

> A talk given in September, 1968,
> at the Buddhist Lecture Hall, San Francisco,
> during the *Shurangama Sutra* lecture series

觀世音菩薩
隨類應現，隨方教化

觀世音菩薩觀一切眾生三世的因緣，然後就
用應當的方法去救度眾生，去教化眾生，
用他所修行成就的這種神通去救度眾生。

觀世音菩薩在佛教裏頭佔很重要的地位。這觀世音
菩薩，有的人說他是中國人，有的人又說他是外國
人；有的人又說他是男人，有的人又說他是女人。
現在我告訴各位，這觀世音菩薩，他也不是中國人
，也不是外國人，他是哪會兒的人呢？他是盡虛空
遍法界，哪個地方都是他，哪個地方也都不是他。
他是隨類應現，應該以什麼身得度的，他就現什麼
身而爲眾生說法，所以他沒有一定的。

這觀世音菩薩他也現佛身來度一切應該成佛的眾生
；他也現菩薩身來度一切應該成菩薩的眾生；他也

Guanshiyin Bodhisattva Manifests Appropriate Forms to Teach Beings Everywhere

Observing the causes and conditions in the three periods of time for each living being, Guanshiyin Bodhisattva employs appropriate methods for saving and teaching that being. He uses the spiritual powers he has cultivated to rescue beings.

Guanshiyin Bodhisattva holds a very important position in Buddhism. Some people say Guanshiyin Bodhisattva is Chinese, while others say he is another nationality. Some people say this Bodhisattva is a man, while others say the Bodhisattva is a woman. Now I will tell all of you: Guanshiyin Bodhisattva is neither Chinese nor any other nationality. Where is he from then? He can be found everywhere throughout space and the Dharma Realm, and yet there is no place where he is. He manifests in response to different kinds of beings, appearing in whatever form is most appropriate to speak Dharma for living beings. Therefore, his appearance is not fixed.

Guanshiyin Bodhisattva appears in the body of a Buddha to cross over all the living beings who are meant to become Buddhas. He also appears in the body of a Bodhisattva in

現天上的天王身來度一切眾生。總而言之，這個眾生應該以什麼身得度的，觀世音菩薩就是現什麼身，來給這一類的眾生說法。

在佛教裏頭，觀世音菩薩各處去教化眾生，要度一切眾生發菩提心。他先看這個眾生歡喜什麼，他先就投其所好；他一投其所好，這個人就歡喜了，所以他說什麼法，這個人也都歡喜聽，於是乎就把這個眾生度了。所以說觀世音菩薩，他也不一定是男身，也不一定是女身；他也是男身，也是女身，不過都是變化的。那麼觀世音菩薩的本體呢？他是如如不動的，和佛是一樣的；並且觀世音菩薩在很久以前，已經成佛了。他的名字叫正法明如來，所以現在他化菩薩身來教化眾生。

在佛教裏他現菩薩身；在外道裏邊，他也現外道的身。所以往往有一個穿著白衣服的，在耶穌教裏就說他是聖母；其實這個聖母是誰？也就是觀世音菩薩去教化那一類的眾生，他去現那麼一個穿白衣服的人的樣子。一般的耶穌教就說這是聖母，其實也

order to cross over all the living beings who are meant to become Bodhisattvas. He also manifests the body of a heavenly king to cross over all living beings. In general, Guanshiyin Bodhisattva appears in whatever form a living being needs to see in order to be crossed over, and comes to speak Dharma for that kind of living being.

In Buddhism, Guanshiyin Bodhisattva goes everywhere to teach and transform living beings. He wants to cross over all living beings and cause them to bring forth the resolve for Bodhi. He first contemplates to see what a living being likes and then caters to his likings. When he caters to that person's likings, the person feels happy and is glad to listen to whatever Dharma he speaks. Thus he successfully crosses over that living being. So I said Guanshiyin Bodhisattva is not necessarily male or female; he is both male and female, but that's just his transformation. In his fundamental identity, Guanshiyin Bodhisattva is thus and unmoving, just like the Buddhas. What is more, Guanshiyin Bodhisattva became a Buddha a long time ago by the name of Light of Proper Dharma Tathagata. Now he is manifesting as a Bodhisattva to come teach and transform living beings.

He appears as a Bodhisattva in Buddhism, but he also appears in other religions as personages of those religions. There is a white-robed figure known in Christianity as the Holy Mother. Who was the Holy Mother in fact? She was just Guanshiyin Bodhisattva coming to teach and transform that class of living beings. He appeared as a person in white robes and the Christians all said that was the Holy Mother,

就是觀世音菩薩，去顯現令這個眾生來發心，無論早晚都會令他明白佛法；明白佛法之後，就發菩提心。這是觀世音菩薩他這種妙用無窮的一種不可思議的境界。

今天我就給各位講一講「觀世音菩薩」這幾個字。

怎麼叫「觀」呢？這「觀」就是一種「觀智」——能觀的智慧；「世音」就是所觀的境界。以這個能觀的智慧，觀這個所觀的境界，觀這個世間所有一切的境界，一切的音聲。這個音聲有苦聲，有樂聲，有善聲，有惡聲，有好聲，有壞聲；觀世音菩薩觀看這世界種種的音聲，他就遂心滿願。眾生無論向觀世音菩薩求什麼，觀世音菩薩一定就遂心滿願的。

「世」，有過去世、現在世、未來世，這三世。觀世音菩薩觀這一切眾生過去世的因緣，現在世的因緣，未來世的因緣，觀看他三世的因緣，然後應該用什麼方法去救度這個眾生，去教化這個眾生，觀

but in fact it was Guanshiyin Bodhisattva appearing to inspire those living beings to bring forth resolves. Sooner and later, they would come to understand the Buddhadharma, and after they understood the Buddhadharma, they would bring forth the Bodhi resolve. That's the inconceivable state of Guanshiyin Bodhisattva's inexhaustible, wonderful functioning.

Today I will briefly explain the name of Guanshiyin Bodhisattva, the "Bodhisattva Who Contemplates the Sounds of the World."

What is contemplation? It refers to a contemplative wisdom, the wisdom that is able to contemplate. The sounds of the world are the state that is contemplated. The wisdom that is able to contemplate is used to contemplate the state that is contemplated—all the states within this world, all the sounds. The sounds include sounds of suffering, sounds of happiness, wholesome sounds, evil sounds, good sounds, bad sounds. Guanshiyin Bodhisattva observes all the various sounds of the world. He fulfills all wishes. No matter what living beings seek from Guanshiyin Bodhisattva, he will grant their wishes for sure.

The Chinese character *shi* (世) for "world" can also refer to "period of time," as in the three periods of time—past, present, and future. Guanshiyin Bodhisattva contemplates the past causes and conditions, present causes and conditions, and future causes and conditions of all living beings. Observing the causes and conditions in the three periods of

109

世音菩薩就用他所修行成就的這種神通去救度眾生，所以這叫「觀世音」。

「菩薩」是半梵語，具足叫「菩提薩埵」，翻譯成中文的意思「菩提」，就是覺；「薩埵」就是有情，就叫覺有情，覺悟這一切的有情。又有一個講法，說是有情裏邊的一個覺悟者。什麼叫有情呢？就是一切有知覺性，有感覺，有氣血的這一些個有生命的東西都叫有情。觀世音菩薩以前和我們是一樣的，就因爲他不怕苦難去修行而覺悟了，是有情眾生裏邊的一個覺悟者。也就是他以他覺悟的這種智慧，再來覺悟我們這一切的眾生，這叫菩薩。

菩薩又有一個名稱叫「大道心的眾生」，他這個道心最大的；有大道心的眾生這就叫菩薩，觀世音菩薩也就是這一類的眾生。

在沒有成佛以前，所有的菩薩也都叫眾生，不過他是眾生裏邊的一個覺悟的眾生，而不是迷昧的一個眾生。迷昧的眾生遇到一切的境界，就執迷不悟，

time for each living being, Guanshiyin Bodhisattva employs whatever method is suitable for saving and teaching that being. He uses the spiritual powers he has accomplished through cultivation to rescue living beings. Thus, he is called the One Who Contemplates the Sounds of the World.

Pusa is an abbreviated transliteration of the Sanskrit word "Bodhisattva" in Chinese. The meaning is translated thus: "Bodhi" means enlightenment and "sattva" means sentient being, so it means "one who enlightens sentient beings," and also "an enlightened one among sentient beings." What is meant by "sentient being"? It refers to any living thing endowed with awareness, sentience, breath, and blood. Guanshiyin Bodhisattva used to be the same as all of us, but because he cultivated without fear of suffering or hardship and became enlightened, he is an enlightened one among sentient living beings. Moreover, he uses the wisdom of his enlightenment to further enlighten all of us living beings. Such a one is called a Bodhisattva.

Bodhisattvas have another name: They are called beings with a great resolve for the Way. They have the greatest resolve for the Way. Beings with a great resolve for the Way are Bodhisattvas. Guanshiyin Bodhisattva is such a being.

Before they become Buddhas, Bodhisattvas are called living beings, but they are enlightened living beings, not confused ones. When confused beings encounter any kind of state, they cling to it and fail to awaken. No matter what situation they come across, they cannot see it for what it is and let go of it. Guanshiyin Bodhisattva is able to see through and let

遇到一切的事也都看不破，放不下。觀世音菩薩對一切的事也都看得破，放得下，無所執著了，所以他覺悟；不但自己覺悟，而且又能去覺悟其他一切沒有覺悟的眾生，所以這叫「觀世音菩薩」。這是觀世音菩薩大概的意思。

一九六八年九月於三藩市佛教講堂
講解《楞嚴經》時

go of all matters. Since he is not attached to anything, he is enlightened. Not only is he himself enlightened, he can also enlighten all other unenlightened beings. Therefore, he is called Guanshiyin Bodhisattva. That's a general explanation of the Bodhisattva Who Contemplates the Sounds of the World.

A talk given in September, 1968,
at the Buddhist Lecture Hall, San Francisco,
during the *Shurangama Sutra* lecture series

觀音菩薩妙難酬

觀音菩薩神通智慧方便，
一切一切的，都是不可思議的。

有一首讚歎觀世音菩薩的偈頌，這是簡略的說觀世音菩薩一個大概。這一首偈頌怎麼樣說的呢？

　　　　觀音菩薩妙難酬，清淨莊嚴累劫修。

說觀世音菩薩他這種神通智慧方便，一切一切的，都是不可思議的。這種不可思議的境界，沒有法子可以講得完。他這種清淨莊嚴的相好，累劫修——不是一生一世修來的，他是生生世世修福修慧。很多個大劫以前，他就修福修慧，才有這種清淨莊嚴的相好，這相貌非常圓滿。

Bodhisattva Guanshiyin Is Wonderful Past Gratitude

Guanshiyin Bodhisattva's spiritual powers, wisdom, expedient means, and everything about her is incredible.

The "Guanyin Praise" gives a general description of Guanshiyin Bodhisattva. How does it go?

> Bodhisattva Guanshiyin is wonderful
>   past gratitude.
> Pure and clear are her adornments,
> Gained through practice ages long.

This describes the inconceivability of Guanshiyin Bodhisattva's spiritual powers, wisdom, expedient means, and everything about her. There is no way to completely express such an incredible state. Her pure, adorned features were gained through many eons of cultivation, not just one life. She has been cultivating blessings and wisdom in life after life, for many great eons. That's why she has such pure, adorned features and such a perfect appearance.

朵朵紅蓮安足下，彎彎秋月鎖眉頭

觀世音菩薩在他腳下有朵朵紅蓮花，他站在紅蓮花的上邊，非常地妙好。彎彎秋月，觀世音菩薩那個眉毛彎彎的，像秋天那個月牙似地鎖眉頭。這個相貌生得非常地妙好，非常地圓滿。

瓶中甘露常遍灑

觀世音菩薩手裏拿著那個淨水瓶，他這個瓶裏所裝的是甘露水。這甘露水向我們每一個人的頭上一灑，我們每個人就得到清涼，災消病散；病也沒有了，災難也消了，罪也滅了，福就會生出來。怎麼叫遍灑呢？遍灑是普遍地，任何人有什麼災難，他都可以去救。

手內楊枝不計秋

觀音菩薩手裏有個楊枝手，他用楊枝沾著甘露水這麼一灑，這個地方就清淨了；什麼魔障也沒有了，什麼麻煩也沒有了，一切一切都清淨了。只要觀世音菩薩來用楊枝沾著甘露水一灑，這個地方就平安無事了。說那楊枝不計秋，就是不知道多少年了。

Sea-vast a red lotus flower
Fragrant rests beneath her foot.
Bay-curve of an autumn moon
Is in the crescent of her brows.

Guanshiyin Bodhisattva has red lotus flowers beneath her feet. She stands upon red lotuses, extremely wonderful and fine. Her curved brow resembles the crescent moon. His appearance is extremely fine and perfect.

Everywhere and constantly,
Sweet dew sprinkles from her vase.

In her hand, Guanshiyin Bodhisattva holds a pure vase filled with sweet dew, which she sprinkles upon our heads, refreshing us and wiping out our disasters and offenses. Our sicknesses disappear, disasters and offenses are wiped out, and blessings are produced. The sprinkling is all-pervasive. She can rescue any person who is in trouble.

In her hand, the willow branch,
Through the countless autumns.

Among the hands of Guanshiyin Bodhisattva, there is a willow branch hand. When she dips the willow branch in sweet dew water and then sprinkles the water, the place is immediately purified. All demonic obstacles and all troubles are gone, and everything is pure and clear. Wherever Guanshiyin Bodhisattva sprinkles sweet dew, that place will be peaceful and untroubled. The willow branch has been there for countless autumns, for who knows how many years.

千處祈求千處應

這觀世音菩薩不是一個地方求，他來救一個地方；你就千處、萬處、百千萬處，有多少人求他，他都遂心滿願，來幫忙這麼多的眾生，令你離苦得樂。

苦海常作度人舟

我們這個世界就好像一個苦海一樣，觀世音菩薩在這個茫茫的苦海裏邊，常常地作度人的這麼一條船的樣子。

觀音菩薩這種的神通妙用、相好莊嚴，講是講不完的。不過我們人知道他一個大概，對觀音菩薩有少少的認識，以後好多接近觀音菩薩，多向觀音菩薩來學習——學習觀音菩薩這種的慈悲，這種的普門示現來教化眾生。

我講到這個地方，想起一個公案來，給大家講一講。這公案本來以前也講過，但是有的人還沒有聽過，不妨給這沒有聽過的人再講一講。

以前在中國的上虞縣有一個商人，就是做生意的。這個商人什麼生意他都做，但是他信觀世音菩薩，

Prayers depart a thousand hearts;
In a thousand hearts she answers.

Guanshiyin Bodhisattva doesn't rescue only one person who is praying to her in one place. However many people pray to him, be it a thousand, ten thousand, or a hundred million, she will answer their prayers. She will rescue that many beings from their woes and bring them happiness.

Sailing the sea of suffering,
Crossing people over.

Our world is like a sea of suffering. In this boundless sea of suffering, Guanshiyin Bodhisattva constantly acts as a ferry to take people across.

One could never finish speaking of the wonderful functioning of Guanyin Bodhisattva's spiritual powers and of her adorned features. However, now at least we have a general idea and know a little bit about Guanyin Bodhisattva, so in the future we will be able to draw near to and learn from Guanyin Bodhisattva. We should emulate Guanyin Bodhisattva's kindness and compassion in manifesting universal doors to teach and transform living beings.

At this point, I will tell everyone a true story that has come to my mind. I've told this story before, but since some people haven't heard it before, I will retell it for their sakes.

Once there was a merchant from Shangyu county of China. This merchant, who engaged in all kinds of trade, believed

很誠心地念觀世音菩薩，拜觀世音菩薩，又念誦這《觀世音菩薩普門品》。有一天晚間，這個商人就作了一個夢，夢見觀世音菩薩來了。觀世音菩薩就告訴他，說：「你啊！將要有一個災難哪。我現在告訴你幾句偈頌；你記得，以後就會應驗。」這個偈頌怎麼說的呢？就說：

> 逢橋莫停舟，遇油即抹頭；
> 斗穀三升米，蒼蠅捧筆頭。

說了這四句，觀音菩薩就不見了。那麼這個商人把這四句也就記得明明白白，很清楚。

有一天，他就裝上很多的貨物，很多的東西到船上，從這一個城市到那一個城市去賣去。這個船在江裏開著，就遇到大雨了。這時正遇到一座橋，好像屋崙橋（奧克蘭大橋）那樣一座大橋。這個擺船的就要把船停到這個橋底下來避雨，不要教雨把東西都打濕了，可是這個商人一想：「哦！說『逢橋莫停舟』，現在在這個橋底下，不要停這個舟啊！」趕快叫這個擺船的，說：「快開船，這個地方不能

in Guanshiyin Bodhisattva, recited Guanshiyin Bodhisattva's name very sincerely, bowed in homage to Guanshiyin Bodhisattva, and recited Guanshiyin Bodhisattva's *Universal Door Chapter*. One night, Guanshiyin Bodhisattva came to him in a dream and said, "A disaster is about to befall you. Remember this verse that I'm going to tell you now, for it will come true in the future." The verse went:

> When you come to a bridge, don't stop the boat.
> When you see oil, smear some on your head.
> One peck of grain yields three pints of rice:
> Flies will cluster on the tip of the brush.

After saying these lines, Guanshiyin Bodhisattva vanished. The merchant remembered the four lines very clearly.

One day, he loaded his boat with many goods, intending to travel from city to city to sell them. As the boat went down the river, it began to rain heavily. Just then the boat was approaching a large bridge, similar in size to the Oakland Bridge. The oarsman planned to stop the boat under the bridge to wait out the rain, so the goods would not get soaked. The merchant thought, "Oh! The Bodhisattva said, 'When you come to a bridge, don't stop the boat.' So we'd better not stop the boat under this bridge!" Then he quickly told the oarsman, "Keep on rowing. We can't stop here."

After they moved the boat out from under the bridge, the bridge collapsed. If it had collapsed when they were still under it, then both they and the goods would have tumbled into the Yangzte River and that would have been the end of

停。」那麼就把船開走。過這個橋之後，啊！這個橋就坍塌了，就壞了。如果他在這橋底下停船的時候，那連人帶東西統統都會打到長江裏頭去，就人連東西都會沒有了。他說：「觀音菩薩眞靈！這回我沒有在這個橋底下停舟，躲過這一個大難。」

他回到家裏更拜謝觀音菩薩。正在拜佛，在佛前點的油燈就跌到地下，把這個油都灑到地下了。啊！他想：「『逢油即抹頭』，這現在是有油了。」所以他把這個油往自己的頭上都抹上了；抹上油了，等晚間休息睡覺，睡到半夜的時候，啊！他聞見有一股血腥的氣——人有血腥氣的；聞見有這麼一股血腥氣，他醒來一看，啊！他太太的頭被人給割下來了。他自己太太被殺了，所以流出很多血，把床都染紅了。那麼在半夜他就趕快去到他太太的父母家裏去報告，說：「今天晚間不知怎麼，你的女兒死了。不知被誰殺的？」

他這岳父、岳母去一看，說：「這誰殺的？一定是你謀財害命。你信佛，你太太不信佛；你們兩個一

them. The merchant said, "Guanyin Bodhisattva is truly efficacious! Since I didn't stop the boat under the bridge, I missed being caught in that disaster."

When he got home, he bowed in gratitude to Guanyin Bodhisattva. As he was bowing, one of the oil lamps on the altar fell down, spilling the oil all over the ground. "Ah!" thought the merchant, "The verse said, 'When you see oil, smear some on your head.' This must be the oil." So he smeared some of the oil on his head. At night, he went to bed and fell asleep.

He woke up at midnight and smelled the rank odor of blood. Becoming wide awake, he took a look—oh! Someone had cut off his wife's head. His wife had been murdered, and all the blood had stained the bedsheets red. At midnight the man rushed over to the home of his wife's parents and reported what had happened. He told them, "I don't know how it happened, but your daughter died tonight. I don't know who killed her."

His parents-in-law went to take a look and said, "Who killed her? You must have come up with this plot to kill her and take her money. You're a Buddhist but your wife wasn't, so you two must have had a difference of opinions. You were upset with her, so you used that pretext to murder her, and then you came and told us." So saying, they reported him to the authorities.

定是意見不相合，你不歡喜她了，藉這個題目把她殺死了。你這麼樣子來報告我。」於是乎就告到縣政府去。

到了縣政府，這個縣官審問，也審問不出所以然來，於是乎就要判這個商人謀殺的罪名成立。正在拿著筆要判這個罪，啊！這很多的蒼蠅就來了，蒼蠅落到這個筆頭上，這個商人就説：「哦！真奇怪啊！這真太奇怪了！這『蒼蠅捧筆頭』。」

那個縣官就問他：「你説什麼奇怪、奇怪的？」他説：「我是信觀音菩薩的。我在家裏作個夢。觀音菩薩告訴我四句話，現在這三句都應驗了，所以我認爲奇怪。」

這個縣官説：「這三句是什麼呢？」他説：「菩薩告訴我『逢橋莫停舟』。我去做生意，這個船到那橋底下，正趕上下雨。這個擺船的要停，我沒叫他停，結果把船開過去那個橋，那橋就坍塌了，壞了；如果我在那兒停舟的話，這個船就被那個橋給砸爛了，連人也都沒有了，這是一樣。他又叫我『遇

124

The county magistrate inquired into the case but could not figure out what had happened, so he decided to pronounce the merchant guilty of murder. As he picked up the brush to write the verdict, a swarm of flies suddenly converged on the tip of his brush, covering the brushtip completely. The merchant said, "Oh! How strange! This is really very peculiar: 'Flies will cluster on the tip of the brush.'"

"What are you talking about? What's so strange and peculiar?" the magistrate asked.

"I believe in Guanyin Bodhisattva. Guanyin Bodhisattva came to me in a dream and told me four lines of verse, three of which have come true. That's why I think it's very strange," replied the merchant.

"How did those three lines go?" asked the magistrate.

The merchant replied, "The Bodhisattva told me, 'When you encounter a bridge, don't stop the boat.' When I was going to sell my goods, my boat passed under a bridge just as it started to rain. The oarsman wanted to stop, but I told him not to stop there. Right after the boat passed under the bridge, the bridge collapsed. If I had stopped the boat there, it would have been smashed to pieces by the bridge and we would have lost our lives. That's one line. Guanyin Bodhisattva also said, 'When you see oil, smear some on your head.' When I was bowing to the Buddhas at home, one of the oil lamps on the altar fell to the ground, spilling the oil.

油即抹頭』；遇到這個油，就自己抹這個頭。我在家裏拜佛，佛前的油燈跌到地下，油都灑到地下了，我就把這個油往自己的頭上抹了。等晚間睡到半夜的時候，我自己太太就被人給殺了。

菩薩又說：『斗穀三升米，蒼蠅捧筆頭。』這『斗穀三升米』，我現在不知怎麼樣？可是現在你這個縣官想要判我罪名，這個蒼蠅來捧筆頭來了。這『蒼蠅捧筆頭』，豈不是也應驗了呢？」

那個縣官一聽，哦！有這麼個事情？現在這三樣都應驗了，就剩一樣，這「斗穀三升米」，就和參謀研究來，研究去，說這一定有一個或者姓米的，或者姓康的，就找這樣一個人，所以就叫密探去到這鄉下一調查，果然有個康七。因為斗穀有三升米，這豈不就是有七升糠，所以就叫康七。

把這個人拿來一問。原來這個人和做生意這個人的太太，有一種不可告人的事情。他們兩個人準備把這個商人殺了，他們好就同住。結果康七這天晚間殺人，他用手一摸，這個商人的頭髮上有油。他說

I rubbed some of that oil on my head. That night I slept until midnight, when I woke up and found my own wife murdered.

"The Bodhisattva also said, 'One peck of grain and three pints of rice: Flies will cluster on the tip of the brush.' I don't know what 'one peck of grain yields three pints of rice' means, but just now when you were going to write out the verdict, all those flies swarmed onto your brush tip. So the line, 'Flies will cluster on the tip of the brush' also came true."

Hearing this, the magistrate thought, "Oh! So that's what's going on. Three lines have come true already, and there's only one left: 'One peck of grain yields three pints of rice.'" He looked into the case with his advisors and deduced that the murderer's surname must be either Mi ("rice") or Kang ("chaff"). A private detective was sent to the village to search for such a person, and indeed, there was a man named Kang Chi. If a peck of grain contains three pints of rice, then there must be seven pints of chaff. And so his name was Kang Chi ("chaff seven").

When the man was brought in for questioning, it turned out he and the merchant's wife had been doing unspeakable things. The two of them had planned to kill the merchant so that they could live together. That night when Kang Chi went to commit the murder, he had felt the oil on the merchant's hair with his hand. He reasoned that the oily hair must belong to the woman—only a woman would grease her hair, not a man—so he beheaded the other

這有油的頭髮一定是女人的；一定是女人頭髮才擦油的，男人不會擦油的，所以把旁邊那個沒有油的那個腦袋就砍下來了。結果這個縣官一問，問明白了，就把康七定罪了。

由此之後，做生意這個人一看：「哦！這世界上的事情，因果很厲害的！」於是乎以後也就出家修道，把這個世間一切一切都放下了。由這一點看來，這觀音菩薩，你只要對他有誠心，他就會有感應的。你有什麼災難，他會幫忙的。

person, the one who didn't have greasy hair. After the county magistrate had questioned him and gotten all the facts straight, he sentenced Kang Chi.

After that incident, the merchant reflected, "Ah! The causes and effects that govern the affairs of the world are really devastating." He then renounced the householder's life to cultivate the Way, relinquishing all worldly things. From this story, we can see that as long as one sincerely believes in Guanyin Bodhisattva, the Bodhisattva will respond. Whenever a disaster happens to you, he will come to your rescue.

播種在西方

什麼叫「作得了主」？
就是不顛倒，不騙自己，
有真正的戒德、定德、慧德。

法界佛教總會於一九六八年成立，金山聖寺於一九七〇年成立，其宗旨是將東方的佛教傳到西方來，並在西方開花結果。西方雖然工業發達，物質文明的水準一直提高，可是生活不斷競爭，令人欲壑難填，所以發生不良的後果。而佛教是提倡精神勝於物質的道理，教人不要自私自利，要學菩薩精神。

《華嚴經》所講的道理就是行菩薩道；《梵網經》所講的，就是守菩薩的戒律，每一條都是爲救眾生，利益眾生，一切爲人不爲己。在這物欲橫流的時代，佛教是起死回生的特效藥。現在菩提種子已經

Sowing Seeds in the West

What does having self-mastery mean ? It means not being deluded and not cheating oneself. It means possessing the virtues of precepts, samadhi, and wisdom.

The Dharma Realm Buddhist Association was established in 1959, and Gold Mountain Monastery in 1970, with the purpose of bringing Buddhism from the East to the West so that it can blossom and bear fruit here. Although Western society is advanced in terms of industry and material comforts, its competitive consumerism creates insatiable desires in people. This leads to an unwholesome outcome. Buddhism emphasizes the importance of spiritual concerns over material ones. It teaches us not to be selfish or concerned with personal benefit, but to learn to be like Bodhisattvas.

The *Flower Adornment Sutra* tells us to practice the Bodhisattva Path, while the *Brahma Net Sutra* speaks of the Bodhisattva Precepts. Every precept is aimed at saving and benefiting living beings; none are for a selfish purpose. In

播種在西方，正在發芽生長中，不久的將來，就會開菩提花，結菩提果，來挽救迷途中的眾生，令其離苦得樂。

在金山聖寺，每個人都要修像真金那樣寶貴的戒力、定力、慧力。三力具足了，將來才能擔當弘法的重任，才能將佛法宣揚於全世界；否則我們一定不能勝任，反而令佛教的前途黯然無光。因此，無論是出家人或在家人都要注意，金山聖寺是專門培養弘法的人才，更是選拔接法人才的好地方。誰能修戒修得真，修定修得真，戒定慧具足圓滿，就有資格做法界佛教總會的主席和金山聖寺的住持。我早想把這兩個職務辭去，請人來擔任，但是多年來一直找不到一位十全十美的人，所以拖延到現在。今天我們要選拔有道德、有學問的善知識，來做金山聖寺的主人。

釋迦牟尼佛曾以以心印心的法門，傳授於摩訶迦葉祖師，迦葉祖師又傳授於阿難尊者。如此代代相傳，傳到二十八祖菩提達摩，他把心法帶到中國來，

modern times when our desires for material things are so overpowering, Buddhism is the wonder drug that can save our spiritual natures. The seeds of Bodhi have already been sown in the West, and now it is time for them to sprout and grow. In the near future they will blossom and bear Bodhi fruit, and the lost and confused living beings will be rescued, so that they can escape suffering and attain bliss.

At Gold Mountain Monastery, everyone should cultivate precepts, samadhi, and wisdom, which are as precious as real gold. With these three kinds of power, we will be able to spread the Buddha's teachings throughout the entire world. Otherwise, if we cannot shoulder the task, the future of Buddhism will be bleak indeed! Left-home people and laypeople alike should pay attention to this. Gold Mountain Monastery specializes in training people to propagate the Dharma. It is the best place for choosing a successor. Anyone who truly upholds the precepts, genuinely cultivates samadhi, and perfects his wisdom is qualified to be the chairperson of Dharma Realm Buddhist Association and the abbot of Gold Mountain Monastery. I have long since wanted to pass these two positions on to someone else, but after all these years I have yet to find a suitable person. Today, we must choose a virtuous and learned good advisor to be the abbot of Gold Mountain Monastery.

Shakyamuni Buddha transmitted the Dharma-door of "sealing the mind with the mind" to the First Patriarch Mahakashyapa, who in turn transmitted it to Venerable Ananda. The Dharma was transmitted from generation to generation in India up to the Twenty-eighth Patriarch

也是一代一代傳下來。到五祖弘忍大師，他將心法、衣缽傳授給不識字的惠能大師。當時傳衣缽的意思，是證明而已，證明這個接法人，是一方的法主，可以教化眾生。其實有衣缽、沒有衣缽，都沒有什麼問題，只要這個人能作得了主，就可以了。

什麼叫作得了主？就是不顛倒，不騙自己，有真正持戒的戒德，有真正修定的定德，有真正智慧的慧德。三德具足，真為佛教貢獻一切，而能弘揚佛法，廣利群生，沒有自私自利的心，絕不為自己打算：「我該怎麼樣在佛教中把名譽造大一點？把地位提高一點？把利益多得一點？」沒有這種思想在作祟，更不會有這種想法：「我要造個大廟，比任何廟都要大；要把齋菜做得美味可口，令居士常來吃齋菜，香油錢源源而來。」我們金山聖寺只想造活佛、活菩薩、活祖師，續佛慧命，替佛教增光。

佛教正統的心法，傳到六祖大師，繼而一華開五葉，成立五宗：溈仰宗、臨濟宗、曹洞宗、雲門宗、法眼宗，一直傳到現在。（按：虛雲老和尚，是溈

Bodhidharma, who took the Mind Dharma to China. In China, the Dharma was also transmitted from patriarch to patriarch. The Fifth Patriarch of China, Great Master Hongren, transmitted the Mind Dharma, plus the robe and bowl, to Great Master Huineng, the Sixth Patriarch, who was illiterate. The robe and bowl symbolized that the recipient of the Dharma was a Dharma Master who was able to teach and transform living beings. Actually, whether or not he had the robe and bowl was not important; what mattered was that he had attained self-mastery.

What does having self-mastery mean? It means not being deluded and not cheating oneself. It means possessing the virtue of precepts that comes from truly holding precepts, the virtue of samadhi gained through genuine cultivation of samadhi, and the virtue of wisdom derived from real wisdom. Being replete with the three virtues, one offers up everything to Buddhism and propagates the Dharma to benefit living beings. One is neither selfish nor greedy for personal gain. One never schemes, "How can I become more famous in Buddhism? How can I reach a higher position and gain more benefits?" Nor does one think, "I want to build the biggest temple. I want to make the best vegetarian food so all the laypeople will come to my temple and the donations will roll in." Here at Gold Mountain, we only want to make living Buddhas, living Bodhisattvas, and living Patriarchs to continue the wisdom life of the Buddha and glorify Buddhism.

The Mind Dharma of Proper Buddhism, after being transmitted to the Sixth Patriarch, split into the five sects of

仰宗第八代祖師，傳法於宣公上人，成爲溈仰宗第九代祖師）我觀察因緣，應該是將心法傳於西方的時候了。

不論出家人也好，在家人也好，誰能終生爲佛教而努力，獻身於佛教，務求佛教發揚光大；有這種志願的人，從今天起限期七天，每個人可以寫一首偈頌，寫出所學的心得，我看看有沒有見性的人。如果有見性的，就是接法人。但不要學神秀大師，急得坐立不安，連飯也吃不下，覺也睡不著了！

一九七四年十月十五日開示

Weiyang, Linji, Caodong, Yunmen, and Fayan, which have been transmitted to the present time. [Note: The Venerable Master Hsu Yun, as the eighth patriarch of the Weiyang Sect, transmitted the Dharma to the Venerable Master Hsuan Hua, making him the ninth patriarch.] Observing the conditions, I saw that it was time to bring the Mind Dharma to the West.

Whether you are a left-home person or a layperson, if you can resolve to devote your life to the propagation of Buddhism, you may write a verse expressing your understanding within the next seven days. I want to see if any one of you has seen your own nature. If so, then you will be my successor. But don't be like Great Master Shenxiu, who was so nervous [when the Fifth Patriarch gave a similar test to his disciples] that he couldn't sit still, eat, or sleep.

A talk given on October 15, 1974

只准正法住世

居士單獨供養一個出家人，
以為有特別功德，
沒想到這是破壞和合僧。

什麼是正法住世？你老老實實去修行，不好虛名假
利，不貪供養，就是正法住世。如果每個出家人能
持銀錢戒，能坐禪，能日中一食，能時刻搭袈裟，
嚴持戒律，就是正法住世。正法住世，也就是時刻
依佛所教，躬行實踐。

你們看看萬佛聖城的出家人，都沒有什麼貪心，每
個人都是默默耕耘，精嚴戒律，肅恭齋法，發大菩
提心。我的願力是無論到什麼地方去，不准末法存
在，只准正法住世。

Perpetuating the Proper Dharma in the World

Laypeople make offerings to a single left-home person, thinking that there is special merit and virtue in doing so, but little do they know that it actually destroys the harmony of the Sangha.

What does it take for the Proper Dharma to exist in the world? If you honestly practice without coveting fame, benefit, or offerings, then the Proper Dharma exists in the world. If every left-home person observes the precept of poverty (not holding money), sits in meditation, eats only one meal a day, always wears the *kashaya* sash, and strictly observes the precepts, then the Proper Dharma exists in the world. The Proper Dharma exists in the world when we practice according to the Buddha's teaching at all times.

Look at the left-home people at the City of Ten Thousand Buddhas. They have little greed, cultivate quietly, carefully observe the precepts, respectfully receive vegetarian meals, and bring forth a great resolve for Bodhi. My vow is that, wherever I go, I will only allow the Proper Dharma to exist; I will not permit the Dharma to come to an end.

末法，就是佛法跑到末梢上、枝葉上，遠離根本了。在末法時期，眞假難分，要具有擇法眼，才可以分辨清楚。什麼是正法？就是不貪名、不貪利、不貪色、不自私。

末法時代的人都是邪知邪見，凡是對的他說不對，不對的他說是對；魚目混珠，正法現前，他也不認識。所以在省庵大師的〈勸發菩提心文〉裏說：「有教無人，邪正不分，是非莫辨，競爭人我，盡逐利名。」

至於競爭人我，他倒有本事，例如，跟人競爭造廟。你的廟高七十呎，我便要蓋一間七十一呎的；你的廟高七十二呎，我便要蓋一間七十三呎的，總要比你的廟高。他不會去比一比較，這個人的修行，是否比我高？修行，他不去比賽；造廟，他卻去比賽。因地不眞，果招迂曲，浪費施主的錢和米，結果領著大家都進了地獄。競爭造廟，有什麼意思？造好後也沒有人住，空空如也，多可憐呀！末法的現象就是這樣。

During the Dharma-ending Age, the Dharma reaches its end, its leaves and branches; it is far removed from the roots. In the Dharma-ending Age, it is difficult to distinguish the true from the false, unless one has Dharma-selecting Vision. To practice the Proper Dharma entails not being greedy for fame and benefits, not lusting after beautiful forms, and not being selfish.

However, people in the Dharma-ending Age have misguided views. They confuse right and wrong, mistaking fish eyes for pearls. Even if the Proper Dharma were presented to them, they would not recognize it. Therefore, Great Master Xing An said in his essay, "Exhortation to Resolve the Mind upon Bodhi," "There are teachings but no adherents. No one can distinguish the deviant from the proper; no one can tell right from wrong. We compete and struggle with each other. We pursue profit and fame."

People in the Dharma-ending Age excel at competition. For instance, they compete in temple building. "Your temple is seventy feet high? I'm going to build one that's seventy-one feet tall"; "Your temple is seventy-two feet high? Then I'm going to build one that's seventy-three feet tall. Mine will always be higher than yours." Instead of comparing to see who excels at cultivation, they compete to see who can build more temples. With such an attitude, they waste donors' money and lead people into the hells. If people do not cultivate honestly, they will get crooked results. What's the point of competing to build temples if no one lives in them? What a pity that we end up with so many empty temples! That's how the Dharma-ending Age is.

還有居士們供養出家人，切記莫生貪心。好像你去護持一個法師，我去護持一個法師，令出家人分開，不能同住修行，這就是破壞僧團。居士們彼此競爭，單獨供養一個出家人，把那個出家人弄得迷迷糊糊，一個人住在小精舍裏，無所事事——到頭來你有什麼功德？

我說的是眞話，出家人應該共同住在大叢林，互相用功辦道，互相警惕策勉。單獨住在小精舍裏，願意不用功，沒有人管；願意吃好東西，沒有人管；願意吃一點肉，喝點酒，都沒有問題。居士們以爲這是功德，其實是幫助那個出家人下地獄哩！你的功德跑到那兒去？我說的話都是大家不喜歡聽的。

你們應該知道：要供養三寶，應該擁護大道場，應該護持眞正修行的地方。不是你佔著一個出家人，我霸著一個出家人，這種事並不如法。我說這番話，很多出家人一定很討厭。爲什麼呢？因爲他不自在了。在大叢林裏，睡覺也不能隨便睡，又不能隨便吃東西，不能開齋破戒。單獨一個人就可以爲所

Laypeople shouldn't be greedy when making offerings to left-home people. If your attitude is, "You support that Dharma Master, and I'll support this one," you are breaking up the Sangha and preventing left-home people from living and cultivating together. If everyone competes to make offerings to a single monk, that monk will become really confused, living in his own little temple with nothing to do. In the end, what merit is there in that?

I am speaking the truth. Monks should live together in a large monastery so that they can cultivate diligently and alert and urge each other on in their practice. If a monk lives alone in a small temple, no one knows when he slacks off in his practice or indulges in good food. It won't be hard for him to eat a little meat and drink a little wine. Laypeople think they are creating merit when they give all their offerings to an individual monk. Actually, they are just sending that monk into the hells! What merit and virtue could the donors possibly attain? The things I say are things that no one likes to hear.

You must understand that if you want to make offerings to the Triple Jewel, you should make them to a large Way-place—a place of true cultivation. It should not be that you make personal offerings to one monk and I make personal offerings to another. That is not in accord with the Dharma.

I am sure many left-home people are annoyed by my words, because I am hindering their freedom. In a large monastery, they cannot sleep or eat casually, nor can they eat meat or break the precepts. Living alone by themselves,

欲爲。當然，也有些人單獨修行，是眞正用功的，但目前來講，這是少之又少的。

爲什麼居士要單獨供養一個出家人？他以爲有特別功德，沒想到這是破壞和合僧。僧是和合眾，就是大家要住在一起修行。你一個人住，怎堪稱和合眾，跟誰和合？老跟在家人和合，就變成在家人了。

我的話是苦口婆心，所謂「忠言逆耳利於行，良藥苦口利於病。」法師不應該是「私家」的，應該是「公家」的。所以金山聖寺、萬佛聖城等道場，常常住很多人，大家彼此勉勵，勸善規過，不是競爭人我。

爲什麼要讚己毀人？因爲貪圖供養。所以勸發菩提心文裏說：「舉目滔滔，天下皆是，不知佛是何人，法是何義，僧是何名？」要四位出家人以上合和相處，方稱爲僧，是和諧共住，無爭無執，單獨一個出家人不能稱爲僧。

they can do whatever they please. Of course there are true cultivators who live alone and work hard at their practice. However, nowadays, such individuals are extremely rare.

Why would laypeople want to make offerings to a single left-home person? They think there is special merit and virtue in doing so. Little do they know that it actually destroys the harmony of the Sangha. The Sangha is a "harmonious assembly"—everyone lives together and cultivates. If you live alone, how can you call yourself a "harmonious assembly"? With whom are you harmonizing? If you are always harmonizing with laypeople, you will end up a layperson yourself.

I am saying this out of deep concern. "Truthful words jar the ear, but help one to act wisely. Good medicine is bitter to the taste, but cures sickness." Dharma Masters should not be privately "owned"; they should be accessible to the public. Therefore, there are always many people living at Gold Mountain Monastery, the City of Ten Thousand Buddhas, and our other temples. They encourage each other, exhort one another to reform, and correct each other's faults. They do not compete against one another.

Why would left-home people praise themselves and slight others? Because they are greedy for offerings. The "Exhortation to Bring forth the Bodhi Resolve" says, "The world is filled with people who don't know who the Buddha is, what the Dharma means, and what a Sangha is." A Sangha refers to a group of at least four left-home people

現在更流行另一種弊病：很多人不單不知道三寶是什麼，有些居士還設立四寶。不是居士們供養三寶，而是要三寶來供養居士。恐怕不久又會發明五寶、六寶、七寶，你看！這不是末法的現象是什麼？

一九七九十一月開示

dwelling together in harmony, with no disputes. One left-home person all by him or herself cannot be called a Sangha.

Another widespread problem is that many people don't know what the Triple Jewel is. There are laypeople who want to set themselves up as a fourth jewel. Nowadays, not only do laypeople fail to make offerings to the Triple Jewel (the Buddha, the Dharma, and the Sangha), they expect the Triple Jewel to provide for them. They may soon come up with fifth, sixth, and seventh jewels. If this is not a sign of the Dharma-ending Age, then what is?

A talk given in November 1979

善知識

什麼是明眼善知識？有四個條件：
不貪錢，不貪色，不貪名，不自私。

要修行，修出世法，必定先要選擇明眼善知識。什麼是明眼善知識？有四個條件：不貪錢，不貪色，不貪名，不自私。應該用這四個條件去衡量善知識，看看他是否說來說去，都是爲了謀自己的利益，或者高舉自己的地位，看看他有沒有私人的企圖？

要親近善知識，不用天天粘著他，而是要聽他的話，聽他的教誨。有問題的時候，可以去請開示；但不是一天到晚都要去見你的師父，才算親近。去時還要必恭必敬地求法，不是連講帶笑，毫不莊重；

A Good and Wise Advisor

Who can be considered a wise teacher with clear vision? There are four criteria: the person isn't greedy for money, fame, or sex, and isn't selfish.

If we want to practice the Dharma for transcending the world, we must select a wise teacher with clear vision. Who can be considered a wise teacher with clear vision? There are four criteria: the person is not greedy for money, fame, or sex, and isn't selfish. We should use these four criteria to determine whether a teacher has wisdom and clarity. We should see whether the person has ulterior motives—does he seek to make a profit or advance his own position, or plotting for his own personal benefit?

Drawing near a wise teacher does not mean hanging around him every day. It means following his teaching. Of course, you can ask for guidance when you run into problems, but you don't have to see your teacher all the time to be "near" him. When you go to see your teacher, you should request instructions in a very respectful manner—not laughing and

也不要為他添麻煩。首先要問他有沒有時間，若有時間，可以請他開示；假設他沒有空，你不能堅持地說：「我必定要見他，我的事情最重要的！」

善知識不會為自己的利益著想。有人問：「萬佛聖城已經很大了，假使為你蓋一個廟，你要不要？」我一定要。「那麼你不是很貪心嗎？」對，我的貪心很大，但不是為我自己，而是為世界佛教建立基本道場，來弘揚正法。所以凡是來到這兒的人，無論你有什麼看法，都是來擁護萬佛聖城。就算你罵也好，譭謗也好，其實都是在幫助萬佛聖城。我不怕人罵，也不怕人譭謗，如果我怕，就不會來美國。無論你怎樣譭謗我，我也覺得很好的。

學佛要多吃虧，永嘉大師說：

> 聞惡言，是功德，
> 此則成吾善知識，
> 不因訕謗起冤親，
> 何表無生慈忍力。

joking and being totally unserious. Don't give your teacher unnecessary trouble. First find out if he is free. If he is, then you can ask for guidance. If he is busy, then you should not persist and say, "I must see him. My business is very important!"

A good teacher never thinks of his own benefit. Some people have asked me, "The City of Ten Thousand Buddhas is already very big. If someone built another temple for you, would you accept it?" I most certainly would. "Well, then, aren't you being greedy?" Yes. I am extremely greedy, but not for my own sake. I want to establish an international headquarters for Buddhism that can propagate the Proper Dharma. Everyone who comes to the City of Ten Thousand Buddhas, regardless of what he or she thinks, is really coming to protect the City. Even if they slander the City, they are in fact helping the City. I am not afraid of being scolded or slandered. I wouldn't have come to America if I were. No matter how much people may slander me, it's perfectly fine with me.

In studying Buddhism, we have to learn to take losses. Great Master Yongjia said,

> Contemplate vicious words as merit and virtue;
> Then vicious words become one's good advisors.
> Do not let abuse and slander arouse enmity.
> How else can one express the power of compassion
>   and patience with the nonarising of dharmas?

有人罵你，是幫助你向好的走，所以要「順逆皆精進，毀譽不動心。」不要因訕謗便起冤恨之心，應該冤親平等，一視同仁；否則怎樣表達無生法忍的慈悲力量呢？

一九七九年十一月六日開示

People who scold us are in fact helping us in our cultivation. Therefore, we must advance vigorously in favorable as well as adverse circumstances, and allow neither praise nor slander to sway us. There is no need to feel resentful when we are slandered. We should treat friends and enemies with equal kindness. Otherwise, how can we express the compassionate strength that arises from patience with the nonarising of dharmas?

A talk given on November 6, 1979

肅恭齋法
飯前三念五觀

不要不知道為什麼吃飯？為什麼穿衣？
為什麼睡覺？迷迷糊糊，得過且過。

出家人用飯前有三念，首先用調羹吃三口湯，每一
口作一念觀想：

第一念是「願斷一切惡」。斷惡，包括吃飯時不生
分別心，不去分別這個有味道，那個沒有味道。有
什麼便吃什麼，不要揀飲擇食，或者打其他妄想。
不要想：「這個地方真不好，吃飯時又不准講話，
很不自由，像坐牢。我來拜佛，還有這麼多規矩，
真沒趣！」

要是這樣想，吃下去也不容易消化。不要總是找人

The Three Recollections and the Five Contemplations Performed at Mealtime

We shouldn't casually go through life in a muddled manner, not knowing why we eat, wear clothes, and sleep.

Left-home people make three recollections before taking their meal. They begin the meal by drinking three spoonfuls of soup, making one recollection with each spoonful.

The first recollection is, "I vow to cut off all evil." This includes not discriminating whether the food is good or not. Just eat whatever food is served. Don't be picky or indulge in idle thoughts as you eat. Don't think, "This place is not nice at all. We're not allowed to talk when we eat, and there's no freedom. It's like being in jail. I only came to bow to the Buddha, and there are so many rules to follow. It's no fun at all!"

If you have such thoughts, you won't be able to digest your food. Don't always look at other people's faults. "If you always see the faults of others, then you haven't put an end

家不對，「常瞅人不對，自己苦未了。」為什麼你不好好地迴光返照，反求諸己？

第二念是「願修一切善」。要發願改過一切習氣毛病。修道就是諸惡莫作，眾善奉行。第三念是「誓度一切眾生」。願一切眾生都能離苦得樂，了生脫死。

吃飯時又應存五觀：

（一）計功多少，量彼來處：先計量自己有何功德來受此供養，又計算農人要經多少勞苦來耕耘這分米糧；應該籌量碗裏食糧的來歷，是很不容易得來的。

（二）忖己德行，全缺應供：忖者，度也。看看自己的德行，是否圓滿了？還是不圓滿？我能夠對得起這缽飯嗎？

（三）防心離過，貪等為宗：戒備己心，離開過非，不生貪念。不是說好吃的就多吃一點，不好吃的

to your own suffering." Why don't you reflect upon and examine yourself?

The second recollection is, "I vow to cultivate all good." We should vow to correct all bad habits and faults. Cultivating the Way is nothing more than "doing no evil and practicing all good."

The third recollection is, "I vow to save all living beings." We vow to help all living beings leave suffering, attain bliss, and end birth and death.

During the meal, we should also make the five contemplations:

1. *Consider the amount of work involved in bringing the food to the table.* Contemplate whether we have the merit and virtue to accept this meal. Then consider how much energy the farmers expended in planting and harvesting the crops. Think about all the different stages of preparation the food went through before it reached our plate. None of it came easily.

2. *Reflect on whether or not one's virtuous conduct is sufficient to entitle one to receive this offering.* Have we perfected our virtuous conduct? Do we deserve to accept this meal?

3. *Guard the mind from transgressions, principally that of greed.* We must watch over our own mind and keep it from errors and greedy thoughts. We shouldn't help ourselves to more of

就不吃。不要揀飲擇食，好吃和不好吃的都是平等，要以此爲宗旨。

（四）正事良藥，爲療形枯：爲什麼要吃飯呢？要把它當做良藥，資助身體。汽車沒有汽油不能走動，人不吃糧食不能生存。吃飯不是爲貪好味，而是爲治飢餓的病。

（五）爲成道業，應受此食：吃飯不是爲了要吃好東西，而是爲了修自己的法身慧命，成就道業。

以上五觀，是吃飯時策勵身心的準繩。其他日常生活上，例如穿衣、睡覺等，也應該一樣。不要不知道爲什麼吃飯？爲什麼穿衣？爲什麼睡覺？迷迷糊糊，得過且過。這些都是最切身的問題，應該了解得一清二楚。

一九七九年十一月七日開示

the good food while not touching food that is not as appetizing. In other words, we shouldn't be picky about food. Whether it tastes good or not, it's food all the same.

4. *Regard the food as medicine to prevent the body from collapsing.* Why do we need to eat? We should regard the food as medicine that provides energy for our bodies. Just as cars cannot run without gasoline, people cannot survive without food. We eat not for the taste of the food but to cure hunger.

5. *This food is taken only in order to accomplish the Way.* We eat not because we want to enjoy good food, but because we want to cultivate our Dharma body and wisdom life to accomplish the Way.

These five contemplations are guidelines to be observed when we eat. They should also be applied to our other daily activities, such as dressing and sleeping. We shouldn't casually go through life in a muddled manner, not knowing why we eat, wear clothes, and sleep. These are all essential matters, and we should understand them very clearly.

A talk given on November 7, 1979

菩提心

發菩提心之後，好像放下麵種，
久而久之，麵便會長大。

什麼是菩提心？我有一個很簡單的比喻：未發菩提心前，好像麵粉未下發粉；一旦發菩提心之後，好像放下麵種。久而久之，麵便會長大。若問菩提心像個什麼樣子？本來它是無形無相，只是個覺道。覺者，覺悟也，就是明白，明白道理。不單是明白，還要修這條道。

也可以用寶塔來比喻菩提心：這一座寶塔，無論它多高多大，必要從地上修起；地，就是我們的心地。要從地上建這座寶塔，使它一層比一層高。菩提

The Bodhi Resolve

Bringing forth the Bodhi resolve is like
adding yeast to the dough, so that it will
rise and expand over time.

What is the Bodhi resolve? I have a very simple analogy:
Before we bring forth the Bodhi resolve, we are like flour
before yeast is added. Bringing forth the Bodhi resolve is
like adding yeast to the dough, so that it will rise and
expand over time. What is the Bodhi resolve like? It is
without any form or mark; it is only the enlightened Way.
To be enlightened means to understand; to understand the
principles of the Way. Yet we should not stop at understanding the principles; we must also cultivate the Way.

The Bodhi resolve can also be compared to a pagoda: no
matter how tall a pagoda you plan to build, you have to
start from the ground. The ground is analogous to our
"mind ground." Just as we have to build a pagoda story by
story from the ground up, the Bodhi resolve is similarly

心，也是從心地上建起，愈發愈大，愈發愈高；本來只是一點點，很小的，但逐漸膨脹、發大；等到功德圓滿了，最後可以成佛。這只是我一個很粗淺的看法，一個簡單的比喻。

一九七九年十一月十二日開示

built up from the mind ground. Starting very small, it gradually grows greater and higher. And eventually, when we perfect our merit and virtue, we will become Buddhas. This is only a very simple and rough analogy.

A talk given on November 12, 1979

殺生食肉的可怕

單是起齋雞、齋鴨這些葷的名字，
裏頭就含有污染的種子。

梁武帝在位時，中國的佛教很興盛，民間凡有婚禮
或喪事，都請和尚去念經。今天時代不同了，現在
只有喪事，才請和尚去念經；遇有喜事，例如結婚
、生子時，卻沒有人請和尚去念經。其實這是錯誤
的，無論紅白事，都應該請出家人念經迴向、種福
，一方面可以超度亡者，一方面可以爲生者增福。

梁武帝時，就有一位誌公和尚，是位高僧，他有五
眼六通，對於前因後果他都一一明了。某次，一個
有錢人家有婚事，便請誌公和尚去念經。他一踏進
門口，便歎息道：

The Horror of Taking Lives and Eating Meat

The mere use of such names as "vegetarian chicken" and "vegetarian duck" plants seeds of defilement.

During the reign of Emperor Wu of the Liang dynasty, when Buddhism flourished in China, people would always invite monks to recite Sutras at weddings and funerals. Times have changed, and now monks are invited to recite Sutras only at funerals. No one asks them to recite Sutras at weddings or baby showers. Actually, this is wrong. Whether it is an occasion for rejoicing or mourning, left-home people should be asked to recite Sutras and transfer the merit, on the one hand to save the deceased, and on the other to increase the blessings of the living.

During Emperor Wu's time, there was a high monk called the Venerable Zhi. Having attained the Five Eyes and the Six Spiritual Penetrations, he could clearly discern causes and effects. One time, a rich man asked him to recite Sutras at a wedding. Upon entering the house, he sighed and said:

> 古古怪，怪怪古！孫子娶祖母。
> 女吃母之肉，子打父皮鼓。
> 豬羊炕上坐，六親鍋裏煮。
> 眾人來賀喜，我看真是苦！

這是什麼意思呢？「孫子娶祖母」，你說怪不怪？原來，這位祖母在臨終時，她拉著孫兒的手，心裏很捨不得，她說：「你們都成家立業，惟獨我這個小孫兒，沒有人照顧。唉！怎麼辦呢？」說完便去世了。

她到了地府，閻羅王便判她：「你既然這樣寵愛孫兒，還是回去做他的妻子，好照顧他。」於是，祖母便托生來做孫子的太太。所以世間上的前因後果，有時是很可怕的。

「女吃母之肉」，在外面，一個女孩子正在吃豬蹄，吃得津津有味，這隻豬原來是她前世的母親。「子打父皮鼓」，誌公和尚再看看那些奏音樂的，打鑼鼓、吹喇叭、吹笛子，好不熱鬧！有個人用力地

How strange! How very strange indeed!
The grandson marries the grandmother.
The daughter is eating her mother's flesh,
And the son is beating on a drum
  stretched with his father's skin.
Pigs and sheep are sitting on the couch,
And the six kinds of relatives are cooking in the pots.
People have come to offer congratulations,
But I see that it is truly suffering!

What does this mean? *The grandson marries the grandmother.*
Would you say this is strange or not? Right before she died,
the grandmother of the family had held her grandson's
hand, not being able to part with him. She said, "You all
have your own families, but this little grandson of mine has
no one to take care of him. Ah! What is there to be done?"
Then she died.

When she arrived at King Yama's court, King Yama gave
her the following verdict, "Since you love your grandson so
much, you might as well go back to be his wife and take
care of him." And so the grandmother was reborn as her
grandson's future wife. The workings of the law of cause
and effect in this world can be quite frightening.

The daughter is eating her mother's flesh. Outside the house, a
girl was eating a pig's foot with great relish, not realizing
that the pig had been her mother in its previous life. *And the
son is beating on a drum stretched with his father's skin.* Venerable Zhi then took a look at the musicians who were beating
drums and blowing on their trumpets and flutes. What

打鼓，鼓是驢皮造的，而這驢竟然是他前世的父親啊！

誌公和尚再往炕上看看，便說：「豬羊炕上坐」，往菜鍋裏一看，便說「六親鍋裏煮」。原來，從前被人宰的豬呀、羊呀，現在都回來吃人，要這些人償還宿報；以前專吃豬羊的六親眷屬，現在反而回來受人烹割，在鍋子裏還債。

「眾人來賀喜」，大家都以爲這是喜慶之日，但誌公和尚只歎息：「我說眞是苦！」其實是人以苦爲樂呀！

大家聽了這段公案後，應該知道殺生食肉的可怕。。我們又研究這個「肉」字：

> 肉字裏邊兩個人，裏邊罩著外邊人，
> 眾生還吃眾生肉，仔細思量人吃人。

所以，能夠茹素是最好。但吃齋時，不要再起什麼齋雞、齋鴨、齋鮑魚等名字。既然吃齋了，爲什麼

excitement! One man was banging away vigorously on a drum stretched with mulehide, not knowing that the mule had been his father in a previous life.

Venerable Zhi looked at the people sitting on the couch and said: *Pigs and sheep are sitting on the couch.* Then he looked in the pots and said: *And the six kinds of relatives are cooking in the pots.* All the former pigs and sheep that had been slaughtered before were now getting even and eating the people who had eaten them before! The six kinds of relatives who had eaten those pigs and sheep were now being chopped up and cooked in the pots to pay off their debts.

People have come to offer congratulations, / But I see that it is truly suffering! Everyone thought it was a happy occasion, but the Venerable Zhi only sighed and said, "This is really suffering!" People take suffering to be joy!

After hearing this story you should understand the horror of killing and eating meat. Let us look at the Chinese character for meat (肉).

Two people (人) are inside the character for meat (肉).
The person inside is linked to the one outside.
Living beings eat the flesh of living beings.
If you really think about it, it is people eating people.

Thus it is best to be vegetarian. However, we shouldn't use names such as "vegetarian chicken," "vegetarian duck," and "vegetarian abalone" for vegetarian dishes. If we are vegetarians, why can't we forget about meat? The mere use

還放不下？單是起這些葷的名字，裏頭就含有污染的種子。所以以後不要再用葷名去講齋菜。

這次有些人到萬佛聖城之後，發願回去要吃長素。這很好，與六道輪迴斷絕往來，你不吃他，他不吃你；你不殺他，他不殺你，這樣便把循環業報清淨了。

又有人問：吃齋有什麼好處？

我說：「沒有什麼好處，是活著上當。」什麼意思呢？因為齋菜沒有肉類那麼好味道，所以說活著上當。可是，假設你不吃齋，便是死了上當。就像一個秤，那一邊重，那一邊輕，你自己去研究研究。

為什麼說吃肉是死了上當？無論你吃什麼東西，便有那種成分在你身上。你吃菜，便有一股菜味；吃蔥，便有一股蔥味；吃牛奶，便有一股牛奶味；吃起士，身上便有一股起士味；吃大蒜，呼吸氣都有大蒜味。因為你所吃的東西，要與你合股，合而為一，變成你身上的一部份。你吃什麼吃多了，身體

of such names plants seeds of defilement. Vegetarian dishes shouldn't be called by non-vegetarian names.

Some people who came to the City of Ten Thousand Buddhas this time have vowed to become lifelong vegetarians. This is a very good thing, because this way one severs unwholesome affinities with living beings in the six paths. If you don't eat them, they won't eat you; if you don't kill them, they won't kill you. The cycle of karmic retribution will thus be purified.

"What benefits are there in being vegetarian?" someone asked.

I said, "There aren't any. You're taking a loss while you're alive." Because vegetarian food isn't as tasty as meat, you take a loss by being vegetarian during your life. However, if you don't keep a vegetarian diet, then you will take a loss after death. It's like a scale. You have to figure out for yourself which side is heavier and which is lighter.

Why will you take a loss after death if you eat meat? Well, your body is composed of the foods you eat. If you eat vegetables, you will smell like vegetables; if you eat onions, you'll smell like onions; drink milk, and you'll smell like milk; eat cheese, and you'll smell like cheese. If you eat some garlic, your breath will smell of garlic. The things you eat become part of your body. If you eat a lot of a certain thing, your body will become very similar to it. Therefore, if you eat a lot of pork, you will become a pig. Eat a lot of beef,

就會變成和它一樣。因此，吃豬肉多了，便會變豬；吃牛肉多了，便會變牛，這是合乎科學和邏輯學的。你的身體和肉類變爲合夥公司；死了之後，也會變成那樣東西。比如，死後要是周身一股豬味，閻羅王嘟嘟鼻子，便說：「你這樣臭，還是去做豬好了。」羊牛雞犬，也都是同一個道理，所以說是死後上當。

你仔細研究，殺豬的人，他的眼睛像豬。爲什麼？他曾經被人殺了好多次，現在他回來報仇了，但眼睛還是豬眼睛；宰牛的人，眼睛像牛眼睛。其實因果是絲毫不爽的，所以說：

千百年來碗裏羹，怨深似海恨難平，
欲知世上刀兵劫，細聽屠門夜半聲。

一碗肉湯裏邊含藏的怨恨，像海那樣深，說不盡的。要知道世上爲何有戰爭、殺戮，譬如兩國彼此戰鬥，死傷連城，這就是眾生的惡業共聚，同時受報。假設你能細聽夜半屠房裏悽屬的叫聲，你便應該明白殺殺不已的恐怖。

and you will become a cow. This accords with science and logic. The meat you eat incorporates with your body, and after you die you turn into that kind of animal. If you smell like a pig, for instance, after you die King Yama takes a sniff and says, "You smelly thing, you should be reborn as a pig." The same goes for sheep, cows, chicken, and dogs. That's what I mean by being cheated after death.

You can investigate this carefully. Why does a butcher of pigs have eyes resembling those of a pig? It's because he had been slaughtered as a pig many times in the past, and now he has come to seek revenge. Although he is human, his eyes are those of a pig. Cattle butchers have the eyes of a cow. The law of cause and effect is never off. There is a verse:

> For hundreds of thousands of years,
> The stew in the pot has boiled up
> A resentment very hard to level.
> If you want to know why
> There are wars in the world,
> Just listen to the haunting cries that come
> From a slaughterhouse at midnight.

The grief and hatred brewed up in a pot of meat stew is as deep as the ocean. It could never be fully described. The wars and massacres in the world are brought about by the convergence of the evil karma of living beings, causing beings to undergo retribution at the same time. If you listen carefully to the cries of misery coming from a slaughter-house in the middle of the night, you will realize the horror of the ceaseless killing that goes on in there.

目前科學已經研究出來，人多吃肉，很容易生癌症。這是因爲動物體上的怨，在你身上積聚多了，久久而久之便變成害人的毒素。因此我們應該與眾生斷絕因果，不要與牛羊雞犬互造罪孽，便能慢慢地把世界上的惡氣轉過來。

在萬佛聖城，我一邊行持正法，一邊要把世上的殺劫轉變過來，無形無相地把它慢慢消滅了。所以我主張人不殺生、不偷盜、不邪淫、不妄語、不喝酒、不吃麻醉藥。最低限度要守五戒，而且還要守得清淨。你們既已到了寶山，不要空手而歸！

一九七九年十一月二十日開示

Scientists have discovered that people who eat a great deal of meat tend to get cancer. This is because the resentful energy in the bodies of slaughtered animals accumulates in the bodies of those who eat meat and eventually turns into a harmful toxin. We should cut off this relationship of causes and effects with animals and stop the vicious cycle of creating offenses against cows, sheep, chickens, and other animals. Then we will gradually be able to lessen the inauspicious energy in the world.

At the City of Ten Thousand Buddhas, we want to uphold the Proper Dharma and avert the crisis of killing in the world. We want to slowly and imperceptibly avert this disaster. Therefore we advocate: not killing, not stealing, not engaging in sexual misconduct, not lying, not drinking, and not taking drugs. At the very least, we should observe the Five Precepts and maintain our purity in that regard. Since you have come to this treasure mountain, don't leave empty-handed!

A talk given on November 20, 1979

修行要及時

沒有人心裏惦念佛菩薩多辛苦，
只懂得為自己子女勞碌奔波。

我們眾生與佛的一念真心，是無二無別的。為什麼佛早已成正覺，而我們仍然輪迴六道，昏迷顛倒，整天愛呀、愛呀愛的，情情愛愛，丈夫也放不下，妻子也放不下，子女也放不下，終日在六塵裏轉。

學佛他沒有看得那麼重要，家庭卻看得那麼重要，總是說：「我要負我的責任。」到你死了，誰來負你的責任？簡直不懂得算數。知道應該修行，便去修行，為什麼要管這麼多閒事？

經文上說：「而佛世尊卻具無量神通智慧。」有神通就是有智慧，智慧駕御神通，神通和智慧是二而

The Importance of Cultivation

Instead of thinking about how hard the Buddhas and Bodhisattvas work, we only know how to toil for our children.

The true mind of living beings is no different from that of the Buddha's. How come the Buddha has accomplished proper enlightenment, while we are still transmigrating in the six paths? Why are we still muddled and confused, obsessed with love all day long, unable to relinquish our attachments to our spouse and our children? Why are we always caught up in the six kinds of sense perception?

Some people regard their families as far more important than studying Buddhism, and they always say, "I have my responsibilities." Well, when you die, who is going to take care of your responsibilities? Your attitude shows a confusion of priorities. If you realize that you should cultivate, just cultivate. Why have so many unnecessary concerns?

A Sutra says: "The Buddha, the World Honored One, has

不二。你若沒有智慧，也不會有神通，此乃是由功德莊嚴的。

「而我等則但有無量業繫煩惱」，你想一想，一生中跟這個有關係，跟那個也有關係，所以被業力纏縛。昔日妄造業緣，今時則被業力所牽，你想脫離三界，業力卻不肯放過你。善惡夾雜業，淨染夾雜業，人我夾雜業，是非夾雜業，統統來了。人被煩惱所障，生死所縛，所以終日迷迷糊糊。

你想要修行嗎？「未到時候哩！」

你想修行嗎？「多等一會吧！」

總是拖延：「等多幾年，小孩子長大了才算。」

「多等幾年，孩子結了婚才算。」

「等我見到孫子才說吧！」

「等孫子結了婚才算。」

「我還未看到曾孫哩！」

這樣那裏有完的一天？你們不要被世上虛假的快樂迷住了，所謂

infinite spiritual power and wisdom." Spiritual power is itself wisdom. Wisdom guides spiritual power. Spiritual power and wisdom are two, and yet not two. If you lack wisdom, you will not have spiritual power either. These come from the adornment of merit and virtue.

"Living beings have only infinite karmic bonds and afflictions." With careful reflection, we'll see that our various relationships with people are actually karmic entanglements. Having recklessly created karmic affinities in the past, we are now dragged about by our karma. We may want to escape the Triple Realm, but our karma will not let us. We have a mixture of good and bad karma, pure and defiled karma, karma of self and of others, and right and wrong karma, and it all comes forth. Hindered by our afflictions and caught up in birth and death, we pass our days in confusion.

Do you want to cultivate? "The time isn't right."

Would you like to cultivate? "I'll wait a little while."

You keep procrastinating: "I'll wait a few more years until the children have grown up."

"I'll wait a few more years until the children are married."

"I'll wait until I see my grandchildren."

"I'll wait until the grandchildren are married."

"I haven't seen my great grandchildren yet."

When will it ever end? Don't be taken in by the false happiness of the world. It is said,

> 名利小事人人好，
> 生死大事無人防。

很多人又怕子女沒有錢用，於是拚命地為子女打天下，結果：

> 財也大，產也大，後世子孫膽也大，
> 天下事兒都不怕，不喪身家不肯罷。
> 財也小，產也小，後世子孫膽也小，
> 些些事兒自完了，子孫產小禍也少。

給子孫留錢愈多，愈容易惹出大禍；給子孫留錢不多，反而沒有這麼多麻煩。所以又說：

> 有子強如父，留財做什麼？
> 有子不如父，留錢做什麼？

有子女比你更有本事，你留錢給他做什麼？子女若不如父，留錢給他，讓他去吃喝嫖賭，放逸無度，反而累了他。

Fame and benefit are trivial,
But everybody craves them.
Birth and death are important,
Yet no one guards against them.

Many people worry that their children won't have money to spend, so they struggle to build an empire for them. The result:

When one has great wealth and property,
One's descendants will have great nerve:
Not afraid of anything under the sky,
They won't stop until they have destroyed
themselves and their families.
When one has little wealth and property,
One's descendants will not be so bold.
Petty problems are easily solved;
With modest assets, they will suffer few calamities.

The more money we leave to our children, the easier it is for them to bring great misfortunes upon themselves. The less money, the fewer the problems. It is also said,

If the son is more capable than the father,
What need is there to leave him wealth?
If the son is weaker than the father,
What's the use of leaving him money?

If your child is capable, why should you leave him money? If your child is weak, leaving him money only harms him, for he will use that money to eat, drink, be promiscuous, and gamble, generally leading a dissipated life.

「心性是一，迷悟天淵」，我們的心性和佛本是一體，迷與悟卻有天淵之別。「靜然思之，豈不可恥？」我們只懂得掛兒掛女，不會掛佛掛菩薩。沒有人心裏惦念佛菩薩多辛苦，只懂得爲自己子女勞碌奔波，供他們讀大學，考博士學位，將來出人頭地，做個大老闆，那時候我有私家車出入，吃得好，住得好，盡情享受。

「修德有功，則性德方顯。」當你修行有德時，什麼智慧、神通都自然顯現出來。所以說：

> 聰明乃是陰騭助，
> 陰騭引入聰明路。
> 不信陰騭使聰明，
> 聰明反被聰明誤。

陰騭，就是人家見不到的功德，無形無相的好事，例如你默默地幫助他人，不要人知道，不願居功。所謂：

> 善欲人知，不是眞善，
> 惡恐人知，便是大惡。

"Although the nature of the mind is basically the same, delusion and enlightenment are as far apart as the sky and a deep abyss." Our minds are essentially the same as that of the Buddha. However, our delusion is worlds apart from the Buddha's enlightenment. "Quietly reflecting upon this, shouldn't we feel ashamed?" We are mindful of our sons and daughters, but not of the Buddhas and Bodhisattvas. Instead of thinking about how hard the Buddhas and Bodhisattvas work, we only know how to toil for our children, sending them to universities so that they can earn doctorates and become super-achievers and high executives in the future. Then we will have chauffeured cars, gourmet food, fancy mansions, and all the luxury we could wish for.

"When you accomplish the cultivation of virtue, the virtue of your nature will manifest." When you have virtue in your cultivation, your inherent wisdom and spiritual power will spontaneously manifest. There is a saying:

> Intelligence is aided by hidden virtue.
> Hidden virtue brings about intelligence.
> People who do not believe in hidden virtue
> Will be hindered by their own intelligence.

Hidden virtue refers to acts of merit and virtue done anonymously—invisible good deeds. This means secretly helping others without taking credit for it. It is said,

> The goodness that we make known
>   is not true goodness.
> The evil that we fear will leak out is great evil.

不用到處去賣廣告，說：「你知道嗎？泰國哪間廟是我造的，新加坡哪座橋是我修的，香港哪個寶塔是我蓋的。」

可是怎麼知道你的錢來歷如何，是否乾淨？或者你偷來、騙來的，那就功不補過了。佛，是你欺騙不來的；不可以造了罪業，然後到廟裏說：「佛老爺，我送你一點錢，賄賂賄賂你，你能消我的罪嗎？」佛不是這樣的。

所以經文上說：「不辜佛化，不負己靈。」就是這個意思。

一九七九年十二月八日開

temple in Thailand, repaired a bridge in Singapore, and built a pagoda in Hong Kong?"

How do I know where you got your money? Is it clean money? Did you steal or cheat to obtain it? If so, your merit and virtue won't be sufficient to wipe out the offenses you committed. You cannot cheat the Buddha. You cannot go to the temple and say, "Lord Buddha, I will give you some money if you eradicate my offenses." The Buddha doesn't take bribes.

Therefore, a Sutra says, "Don't disappoint the Buddha, and don't let yourself down."

A talk given on December 8, 1979

我們活著為什麼？

我們永遠都應該以利人為前提。
利人，就要從從不障礙人開始做起。

我們活著為什麼？這個「我」是誰？是你、是我，
也是他；可是我們來到這個世界，又為了什麼呢？

有人說：「收拾垃圾！」是這樣嗎？可是現在的人
，是專門撿前人的垃圾，還自以為是寶貝；盡去學
別人的樣子，卻漠視自己本地的風光，還自己給自
己辯護，說：「不學別人的樣子，那別人的樣子，
又從哪裏來？」這就是捨本逐末，頭上安頭，好像
東施效顰一樣，自己真實的智慧遮蔽了，不懂得去
開發，卻盡去向外馳求，結果愈跑愈遠。這種人真
是大錯特錯！

What Are We Living for?

We should make it our top priority to benefit others. The first step in benefiting others is not to obstruct others.

What are we living for? Who are we? What are we here for?

Someone says,"We're here to collect garbage." Is that so? Nowadays, people pick through things that others throw away, finding treasures in others' garbage. People also plagiarize and copy others' styles, while neglecting their own inherent talents. They rationalize, "If copying isn't allowed, then where did other people get their styles from?" They renounce the essence and grasp at trivialities, making things worse by clumsily trying to imitate others. As a result, their own true wisdom remains concealed and undeveloped. The more they direct their attention outwards, the further away they drift! This is truly a great mistake.

But why are we born here? To pan gold and seek profit? No! To make fortunes? No! Money and material things are not truly useful. When the time comes to die, what use are they?

那麼我們人生在這個世界，又爲了什麼呢？爲了淘金年利嗎？不是！爲了賺錢發財嗎？也不是！金銀財寶都不是實在的，等到人死了，這些又有什麼用呢？

既然這樣，那我們人活著，究竟爲了什麼？我們人生在這個世界上，應該有功於世，有德於民，利益一切的眾生，這是我們的責任。不要看輕自己生命的意義，以爲人只是爲了謀求個人的利益。我們應當爲全人類做著想，我們永遠都應該以利人爲前提。什麼是利人？利人，就要從不障礙人開始做起；損人利己，惱害他人，都不是我們應該做的事。

所以我們人生在這個世界上，應該以立功、立德爲本；至於立言，那是其次了。因爲功和德是沒有形相的，而言語是有形有相的。所謂「言語道斷，心行處滅。」我們如果能做到這樣，可以說離道就不遠了。

一九八〇年三月廿一日晚間開示於萬佛聖城

What have we come into this world for? Since we have been born here, we should help the world and the people in it. Benefiting living beings is our duty. We shouldn't degrade the value of our life by directing it towards selfish ends. We make it our top priority to benefit others and always be concerned about humanity as a whole. The first step in benefiting others is not to obstruct others. To benefit ourselves at the expense of others, thus bringing harm and affliction to others, is not a proper thing to do.

Being born in this world, our first task is to establish merit and virtue; writing literature is secondary. Merit and virtue are invisible, while words are visible. It is said, "When words are cut off, the mind's activity ceases." If we arrive at that state, we are not far from enlightenment.

A talk given on the evening of March 21, 1980,
at the City of Ten Thousand Buddhas

浩劫能改變嗎？

本來定業不可轉，
但是三昧加持力，能消除無量罪業。

修道的人，首先不要自私。這不單是爲了保護自己，也是爲了要饒益全世界。我們要把自己放下，不是想：「我怎樣怎樣了不起？」而是要顧全大局。

胡大川先生的「幻想詩」裏，有幾句說得很好：

> 浮沉道力未能堅，
> 世網攖人只自憐；
> 四海應無極樂國，
> 九霄豈有寄愁天。

190

Can Catastrophes Be Averted?

Although it's said that fixed karma cannot be altered, with the power of samadhi even limitless offenses can be dispelled.

Cultivators should not be selfish, nor should they act only to protect themselves. They should work to benefit the whole world, putting personal interests aside. Instead of being enthralled with their own achievements, they should consider the big picture.

Mr. Dachuan Hu's "Fantasy Poem" says it well:

> Bobbing up and down,
> We lack a strong resolve for the Way.
> Caught up in worldly entanglements,
> We feel sorry for ourselves.
> There is no paradise within the four seas;
> What place is there in the nine heavens
> To set our sorrows aside?

「浮沉道力未能堅」，我們人在世界裏浮沉不定，做善功德，便向上昇；造惡業的，便往下降。這樣一浮一沉，生生世世在業海裏漂流，被世事的波濤所動搖，很不容易立得住。

「世網攫人只自憐」，世間法就好像一個大羅網，把所有人都絪住了。愛名的便被名網所絪，貪財的便被財網所纏，迷色的便被色網所縛。總而言之，被財、色、名、食、睡五欲之網，支配得顛顛倒倒，纏縛得透不過氣來。只自憐，一般不明白的人，雖然被網所絪，還不知不覺；明白的人雖然知道，卻沒有法子脫離，只是徒增感歎而已。

「四海應無極樂國」，舉目四海，找不到一個安樂太平的地方。全世界人類都生活在恐懼之中，朝不保夕，到處都是難民，很多地方缺乏糧食、衣服，到處都有火山爆發、地震、水災、天災人禍，紛至杳來，這怎教人不怵目驚心呢？所以說「四海應無極樂國」。

「九霄豈有寄愁天」，九霄雲外，也沒有一個處所

Bobbing up and down, we lack a strong resolve for the Way. People move up and down in the world; rising when they do good deeds of merit and virtue, and falling when they create unwholesome karma. In life after life, they drift and flounder in the sea of karma; being rocked by the waves of worldly affairs, it is hard to stand firm.

Caught up in worldly entanglements, We can only feel sorry for ourselves. Worldly affairs are like a huge net that binds people up. Fame-seekers are bound by the net of fame; money worshippers get caught in the net of wealth; and promiscuous individuals are trapped in the net of lust. In general, the net of the five desires—for wealth, sex, fame, food, and sleep—confuses people and binds them so tightly that they can hardly breathe. Most people don't even know they are caught in the net, and those who do cannot escape, so they can only sigh in self-pity.

There is no paradise within the four seas. Look around: you won't find a peaceful place anywhere. All of humankind lives in fear from dawn to dusk. There are refugees everywhere. In many places people lack adequate food and clothing. Volcanic eruptions, earthquakes, floods, and other natural and manmade disasters happen one after another. How could one not feel scared?

What place is there in the nine heavens to set our sorrows aside? There isn't any space within the nine heavens to store our

來積存這麼多憂愁，因爲放不下這麼多！在這世上，有些人認爲是很快樂，其實是水深火熱的樊籠。水深會把人淹死，火熱會把人燒死，有什麼值得留戀呢？

大家都知道最近華盛頓州的聖海倫火山爆發了，熔岩若堆起來，可以積疊成十二英哩那麼高，灰塵遍灑到四面八方。由此觀之，世上哪有安樂國呢？生在這個危險的多難之秋，各位應該趕快發菩提心，求無上道！

加州爲什麼沒有火山爆發的災難？因爲這裏信佛的人比較多，佛教的道場也較多，所以無形中使災難化爲吉祥。在一九六八年，美國的天文學家、歷史學家、預言學家、科學家，都互相印證，認爲那年三藩市必定會發生大地震，甚至整個三藩市會掉進太平洋！話雖如此，可是僥倖當年並沒有地震。隨後每一年都傳出地震的預言，但每一年都沒有大地震。可是最近地震恐怕眞地快要降臨了，爲了這個原因，法界佛教總會、萬佛聖城、金山聖寺、如來

cares and worries. Some people think the world is a happy place, but actually, we are in danger of being drowned or burned at any moment. Why should we be so attached to this world?

You have all heard of the recent eruption of Mount Saint Helens in Washington State. If the lava were piled up, it could reach as high as twelve miles. The ashes have scattered everywhere. From this eruption we can see how unsafe the world is. Living in these dangerous times, we should quickly bring forth the Bodhi resolve and seek the supreme Way.

Why haven't there been any volcanic eruptions in California? One reason is that there are more Buddhists and more temples here. Disasters are imperceptibly transformed into auspiciousness. In 1968, astrologers, historians, prophets, and scientists in the United States all predicted that a major earthquake would occur in San Francisco that year. They said the earthquake would be so great that the entire city of San Francisco would fall into the Pacific Ocean. Fortunately, no earthquake occurred despite their predictions. There have been earthquake predictions every year since then. However, the great one hasn't happened yet.

Recently, I have been worrying that the earthquake is really going to happen. That's why the fourfold assembly of the Dharma Realm Buddhist Association at the City of Ten

寺及法界佛教大學的四眾弟子，除了每天的早晚課之外，每逢週六都集體誦持〈楞嚴咒〉，藉以祈禱消災解厄，遇難呈祥，化地震於無形，使大的難化爲小，小的化爲烏有。

有人問：這種浩劫能改變嗎？當然可以改變！本來定業不可轉，但是三昧加持力，能消除無量罪業。

一九八〇年六月開示

Thousand Buddhas, Gold Mountain Monastery, Tathagata Monastery, and Dharma Realm Buddhist University has gathered together to recite the Shurangama Mantra on Saturdays. With the power of the mantra we hope to avert the earthquake, dispel danger, transform big disasters into small ones, and make small ones disappear altogether.

Someone is asking, "Can catastrophes be averted?" Of course! Although it's said that fixed karma cannot be altered, with the power of samadhi even limitless offenses can be dispelled.

A talk given in June 1980

認識自己本有的家珍

一般人只懂得求假的，而忘卻真的。

胡大川先生在幻想詩裏，又有幾句說得很好：

> 生不願為上柱國，死更不願作閻羅；
> 閻羅點鬼心殘忍，柱國憂民事更多。

他說：我活著的時候不願意做上柱國（宰相），死後更不願做閻王爺。為什麼？閻羅王很殘忍，他一發脾氣便把這個小鬼投到油鍋裏，又把那個小鬼拋到刀山上。他這樣殘忍，所以我死後不願做閻羅王。宰相呢？時刻憂國憂民，沒有一刻空暇，我也不願意當這個差事。還是好好地修心養性，涵養玄德

Recognizing Our Inherent Treasures

Ordinary people seek after the false and forget about the true.

Mr. Dachuan Hu has a few more lines in his "Fantasy Poem," which states things quite well:

> I don't wish to be a prime minister in life,
> Nor do I wish to be King Yama after I die.
> King Yama is cruel in sentencing the ghosts,
> And a prime minister is too busy worrying
> about his people.

He said, "While I am alive, I have no ambition to be a prime minister, and after I die I don't want to be King Yama. Why? King Yama is very cruel. When he gets angry, he dumps this little ghost into the pot of boiling oil and throws that little ghost onto the mountain of knives. I wouldn't want the job of a prime minister either, for he has to worry constantly about national affairs and has no time to rest. It's more practical for

，更爲實用！所以在這首詩上，又有兩句：

> 但願百年無病苦，
> 不致一息有愁魔。

胡大川先生又爲那些好酒、色、財、氣之徒，作一個生動的寫照。

好色的人就打這個妄想：「好花常令朝朝艷」，好色的人最喜歡花常年開得燦爛，爭妍鬥麗，永不凋謝。這好比一個人願望他的妻子青春常駐，永不衰老；或者有人希望自己的丈夫永遠少年英俊，頭髮不白，皺紋不生，是同一個道理。

好氣的人打這個妄想：「明月何妨夜夜圓」，這個人說：「月圓的晚上雅緻極了，月白風清，星影流光；在園子裏悠閒賞月，好不寫意，爲什麼月兒不能夜夜圓滿？太陽天天都是圓的，爲什麼月兒不能夜夜圓呢，太不公平了！」

好酒之徒又想：「大地有泉皆化酒」，這個人最愛喝酒，於是他便打這個妄想：「假設大地所有的川

me to spend my time cultivating the inner nature and fostering its inherent virtues. The poem also says,

> I hope to be free from illness for a hundred years,
> And not troubled by grief for even one moment.

Mr. Dachuan Hu vividly portrayed those who are fond of wine, beauty, wealth, and fame in his poem.

He said that those who like beauty may wish: *"Beautiful flowers should stay abloom every day.* Flowers should bloom all year round and never wither." This also refers to a man wishing his wife would stay young forever, or a woman wishing her husband would stay handsome and never get gray hair or wrinkles.

People with big tempers may indulge in this wish: *"Why can't the moon be full every night?* It's so nice to sit outside and gaze at the full moon on a night when there is a gentle breeze and the stars are shining. Why can't the moon be full every night, just as the sun is full every day?"

People who like wine fantasize: *"What if all the springs on earth turned into wine?* If all the water in the rivers, streams, ponds, and lakes became wine, I could just reach out and scoop up wine to drink whenever I felt thirsty. Wouldn't that be convenient?"

河池沼都化爲酒泉，那麼每當我渴了，只要伸手往泉裏一汲，便能取美酒來喝，這不是最方便嗎？」好財的人又這樣想，「長林無樹不搖錢」：「假若林中的樹木，統統長滿了鈔票，要用時只須搖搖樹幹，錢便會紛紛而下，這樣不是很省事嗎？」

可是，這都是愚夫愚婦盲目的狂想而已。一般人只懂得求假的，而忘卻真的，都忘了我們的真如自性才是本有的家珍，是取之不盡、用之不竭的。什麼是真如自性？就是每個人本有的佛性。這個佛性，是不生不滅、不垢不淨、不增不減，圓陀陀、光灼灼，在佛的分上沒有增加一點，在眾生分上也沒有減少一點，是如如不動，了了常明的。

可是一般人被自私自利心所蒙蔽，加上嫉妒障礙，心眼變得比一粒微塵還要小，所以只懂得看眼前的，長遠一點的道理便不認識了。爲了這個原因，所以不能返本還原。我們若能

> 悟以往之不諫，知來者之可追，
> 實迷途其未遠，覺今是而昨非。

People who are fond of wealth think: "What if money grew on every tree in the forests? Whenever I needed money, I could just shake the trees and money would fall. That would save me a lot of trouble."

These thoughts are the fantasies of fools. Ordinary people seek after the false and forget about the true. They forget that their inherent true nature is an inexhaustible treasure trove. What is the inherent true nature? It's the Buddha nature within each one of us. The Buddha nature is neither created nor destroyed; it is neither defiled nor pure; and it neither increases nor diminishes. It is perfect and bright; the Buddhas do not have more of it, and living beings do not have less of it. It is unmoving and constantly clear.

Blinded by selfishness, greed for personal gain, jealousy, and obstructiveness, our minds have become smaller than a speck of dust. We see only what is immediately in front of us and fail to understand far-reaching principles. That's why we cannot return to the origin. As the [classical Chinese] poet Tao Yuanming said,

> We should realize that while the past has gone by,
> We can work on the future.
> If we recognize past errors
> And know that we are right today,
> Then we have not strayed too far.

If we realize our past mistakes, we can turn around and reform. To reform and become a new person means getting

我們能夠覺悟以往的過錯，便可以轉過頭來，重新做人。做新人，就是要沒有自私自利心，沒有嫉妒障礙，沒有貢高我慢。

修道人志願在明心見性，不是口頭上說：「我已明了心，見了性，我已經開悟了！」不是單在口頭上用功夫，而是要有真修實證。明心的人，覺得天下任何事也不困難，也不怕苦。為什麼呢？因為他已通達萬物之本體，徹法底源，所以凡事都任運自在。見性的人不憂愁，心如明鏡，又心如止水，事來則應，事去則靜，這就是最實際的證明。人沒有無明煩惱，般若智慧便現前，自然現出自性的大光明藏。

什麼是自性的大光明藏？裏面無人相、無我相、無眾生相、無壽者相；可是，也有人相、也有我相、也有眾生相、也有壽者相。雖然無相而不滅相，有相不礙無相，無相不礙有相，有無自在，有無如如。在這個境界分上，心佛與眾生，是三無差別的。

學佛的人，應該問問自己：「我布施是為了求名，

rid of selfishness, greed for personal gain, jealousy, obstructiveness, and arrogance.

The goal of a cultivator is to understand his mind and see his nature. That doesn't mean simply *saying* that you understand your mind, see your nature, and are enlightened. You must have genuine achievement in your practice; don't just pay lip service. Once you understand the mind, nothing will present any difficulties. You won't fear any hardships. Why not? Because you will understand the essence of all things. You will have penetrated to the source of the Dharma. You will be free and at ease in everything you do. Once you see the nature, you won't have any worries. Your mind will be like a clear mirror or like calm water, reflecting states when they come and becoming still when they pass. This is the most genuine proof of skill. Once ignorance and afflictions are gone, *prajna* wisdom will manifest and the brightness of the inherent nature will shine forth.

What is the brightness of the inherent nature? It's the absence of attachment to the appearances of self, others, living beings, and life span. And yet these appearances still exist. Despite the lack of attachment to them, they are not destroyed. Appearances do not obstruct nonappearances, and nonappearances do not hinder appearances. One is free and at ease between existence and nonexistence. In this state, there is no difference between mind, Buddha, and living beings.

Students of Buddhism should ask themselves, "Am I practicing giving just to make myself look good? Am I holding

還是爲了眞心修行？我持戒、忍辱、精進、禪定、修智慧，是爲了要給人家看，還是爲了眞心修行？」修道不是戴面具，不是裝模作樣，專給人家看的。修道全靠自己用功夫，付出一分功夫，便有一分收穫；拿出一分誠心，則有一分感應。一切一切，都要眞實不虛，切勿自欺欺人！願共勉之。

一九八〇年六月十五日開示

precepts and practicing patience, vigor, samadhi, and wisdom just to show off? Or am I really sincere about cultivating?" Cultivation doesn't mean putting on a show for others. It requires genuine effort. For every bit of effort we put in, we gain a corresponding bit of skill. For every bit of sincerity we muster, we obtain a bit of response. We must be completely true in all we do. We shouldn't cheat ourselves or others. Instead, we should mutually encourage one another.

A talk given on June 15, 1980

糊塗債

以前種下的因，如今結果了，
有什麼好怨呢？

每個人的面目不同，其因果也不一樣，每個人在往昔生生世世所欠下的債也不同。有些人欠的債太多了，到這世界上來，還也還不了，所謂「債臺高築」，也就是業障之臺，一天比一天高，一天比一天深，債上加債，糾纏不清。

這是什麼緣故呢？是因為往昔專門放高利貸，借錢給人，利上加利，貪得無饜，自己以為佔了便宜，結果是自己吃了虧，業障一天比一天重，終於拔不出腿來了！

Confused Debts

Everything in the present is an effect resulting from causes planted in the past. So, what is there to feel resentful about?

Just as each person has unique features, he or she also has unique causes and effects and an individual set of debts incurred in past lives. Some people have such heavy debts that they cannot repay them in one lifetime. Their debts (their karmic hindrances) keep getting higher and deeper with each passing day. Debts are slapped on top of debts until they can never extricate themselves.

Why is this? In previous lives they were loan sharks; they lent money to people at exorbitant interest rates. In their insatiable greed, they thought they were getting a bargain, but in fact they were taking a loss. Their karmic hindrances became heavier and heavier until they finally became stuck.

有的欠人做父親的債，有的欠人做母親的債，有的欠人做妻子的債，有的欠人做丈夫的債，有的欠人做兒子的債，有的欠人做女兒的債。所謂「父母的飢荒，倫常的賬碼」，種種的因緣，乃促成你我今生命運的安排。可是一般人不明白一切都是前因後果，定業難逃，所以有時候還不認賬，還想扛債不還，明明欠人的債，卻不承認。

因為這樣不講道理，所以釀成世界上種種麻煩的發生——你有你的麻煩，我有我的麻煩，他有他的麻煩，各人有糾纏不清、善惡夾雜的因果。偶爾遇到佛教，聽了佛理，便明白一點；可是今天明白了，明天又糊塗了；後天又想明白，大後天又糊塗了。於是變成智愚平等的局面，糊塗時便不想修道，明白時便想修道。可是修道的時候很少，糊塗的時候很多，因此所修的不及所丟的，智慧也一天不如一天，而愚癡卻一天比一天增加，在無明驅使之下，便做出很多糊塗事。心裏糊塗，進一步身上也糊塗了；心裏有貪瞋癡，身上便犯殺盜淫，這些都是糊塗賬，根本算不清！

Some owe the debt of being a father or a mother; others owe the debt of being a husband or a wife; others owe the debt of being a son or a daughter. There is a Chinese phrase, "the debt of being parents in the account-book of human relations." Our fate in this lifetime is determined by various causes and conditions. Ordinary people do not realize that everything is a result of cause and effect and that there is no escape from fixed karma. Sometimes they refuse to acknowledge their debts and pay up. Such unreasonable behavior leads to all sorts of problems in this world: You have your problems, and I have mine. Each person has his or her own set of causes and effects involving a mixture of good and bad deeds.

Once in a while, we may encounter Buddhism and understand a little bit of its principles. One day we may understand, but the next day we become muddled again. The day after that we try to understand again, but the following day we are confused again. There is an equal balance of wisdom and delusion. On days of wisdom, we want to cultivate; on confused days, we don't. Most of the time we are confused, and we spend very little time cultivating. The fruits of our cultivation are far too few to make up for the merit we lose. Our wisdom diminishes and our delusion increases day by day. Driven by ignorance, we do many foolish things. Our confused thoughts lead to confused actions. The greed, anger, and delusion in our minds causes us to commit acts of killing, stealing, and lust. These confused accounts can never be straightened out.

所以有時家庭眷屬不和，父子不和、母女不和、夫婦不和、兄弟不和、姊妹不和、兄妹不和，種種問題就發生了。發生了，自己還不承認、不認賬，反而覺得很受委曲。其實這都是前因後果的定律，以前種下的因，如今結果了，有什麼好怨呢？所以

> 是故知命者，不立巖牆之下，
> 不怨天、不尤人，
> 下學而上達。

首先要明白因果，不要再種糊塗因果，要種清淨的因果，要是道則進，非道則退。不要再把善惡混淆不清，是非夾雜不明，若能黑白分明，真假了然，便有機會返本還原，回復到本有的性淨明體、妙真如性。

一九八〇年六月十六日開示

As a result there is disharmony within families: fathers can't get along with their sons, mothers can't get along with their daughters, husbands and wives don't get along, and brothers and sisters are in disharmony. However, instead of acknowledging the problems and accepting responsibility, each person feels wronged. Actually, all of this is the law of cause and effect at work. Everything in the present is an effect resulting from causes planted in the past. So what is there to feel resentful about? There is a proverb:

> One who understands fate will not stand
>   beside a crumbling wall.
> He neither complains to heaven
>   nor blames other people.
> His subordinates learn from him,
> And his superiors know him.

First of all, we should understand cause and effect. We should plant pure causes and stop planting confused ones. We should advance upon the Way and retreat from what is not the Way. We should not confuse good and evil, right and wrong. If we can distinguish black from white and false from true, then we have the chance to return to the source and recover the pure, bright essence of our wonderful, true, and inherent nature.

A talk given on June 16, 1980

萬物的主宰者

如果真是受神支配的話，
那神就不應該教我們做種種惡，
應該只教我們做種種善。

要知道一切的一切，都是從「一」聚集而成，又要知道多是由很多的「一」而成就的，以前所講的○字，那是超出數外，所謂「超出三界外，不在五行中。」三界就是欲界、色界、無色界，五行就是金、木、水、火、土。

所有的人，都在五行中，每個人的相貌，都具足五行，臉瘦身高，屬於木形；頭尖下巴寬，屬於火形；面方色黃，屬於土形；面白屬於金形；面黑而肥，屬於水形。

The Lord of All Things

If we were ruled by a god, he should keep us from doing evil and cause us to do good.

Everything is formed from the "one." The "many" are formed from the accumulation of many "ones." Earlier I mentioned that the zero is beyond numbers, "beyond the Three Realms and outside of the five elements." The Three Realms are the realm of desire, the realm of form, and the formless realm. The five elements are metal, wood, water, fire, and earth.

All people are included within the scope of the five elements. Our features are characterized by the five elements. For example, tall people with thin faces are predominantly of the wood element. Those with pointed heads and wide chins belong to the fire element. People with squarish faces and yellow complexion are earthy; those with whitish or pale complexions are metal, and those with plump and dark-complexioned faces are of the water element.

有人是木火土，有人是木火金，有的人本身金木相剋，自己和自己鬥爭。水形和火形在一起，木形和土形在一起，便會常發生鬥爭，但○字就超出這些數目之外。

一般人認為命運有一定的安排，所謂「命有八尺，難求一丈。」不錯！但這是指平常人而言，若是修道人，就不在此數中。修道人不要問易經，那是一般凡夫俗子所用的，修道人的生死尚且能了，何況其他的數呢？更應該超出去，所以不要理會這些。

講五行不過明白其理而已，其實認真去修行，什麼道理自然而然就會明白。這個○字是最要緊的法門！各位若對○字用功夫，仔細研究一番，將來一定會有辦法。因為它不在數中，數目一開始，就有個「一」，可是○字，連「一」也沒有了。

要知道「一」多了，就是眾多，眾多是由「一」成就的，所謂

　　一本散為萬殊，萬殊仍歸一本。

　　一為無量，無量為一。

Some people are a combination of wood, fire, and earth; others may be wood, fire, and metal. People who are a combination of the mutually destructive elements of metal and wood often fight with themselves. If water-type people are put together with fire-type people, or wood-type people meet earth-type people, many quarrels and arguments may ensue. However, the zero transcends all these kinds of fate.

Most people think that destiny is fixed. There is a saying, "If something is fated to be eight feet, it's hard to ask for ten feet." This is true, but only for ordinary people. Genuine cultivators aren't bound by fate. Cultivators don't need to consult *The Book of Changes*; that's for ordinary people. Cultivators are able to end birth and death; how much the more can they alter other aspects of their fate. Thus, we should transcend fate and not pay attention to it.

We have discussed the five elements to understand their principles, but in fact, if we earnestly cultivate, we will spontaneously understand all principles. The zero is essential. If we work on it and investigate it, we will certainly find a way. The zero transcends all numbers. The numbers begin with one, but the zero is beyond even the one.

When there are many "ones," it becomes a multitude. The "many" are formed from "one." As it is said,

> *One root spreads into ten thousand branches,*
> *Yet the ten thousand branches return to the one root.*

The one is limitless; the limitless are one.

爲什麼有無量？因爲有一，爲什麼有一？因爲有無量。若是「一」生出來，就有很多麻煩事，從一生出二三四，乃至八九十，無窮無盡的數目就跟著來了；若是「一」沒有了，其他當然也沒有了；眾多微塵空了，一粒微塵也沒有了。

諸法沒有一個自性，所以無所依賴，但是從互相假和合，而成就一切方便法。

天地間一切萬事萬物，有些人說在冥冥中有主宰操縱，這是能作。一切萬事萬物，這是所作。有個主宰它能作一切萬事萬物，一切萬事萬物是它所作出來的，一般宗教，都是這樣說法。可是往眞實來講，沒有哪個人能主宰一切萬事萬物，所以才說無能作所作，沒有一個能作者，也沒有所作。

那是怎樣呢？所有一切的一切，都是起惑、造業、受報。業是從什麼地方生出來？是從妄想所感召出來的。在最初是不覺，不覺就是無明，因爲無明，就生出迷惑。要是沒有無明，就沒有迷惑；有了迷惑，就生出妄想；有了妄想，就造出種種的業。所

How can there be the limitless? Because of the one. How can the one exist? Because of the limitless. Once the "one" comes into being, there are many troubles. From the one comes two, three, four, ... eight, nine, ten, and all the numbers up to infinity. Without the "one," the other numbers cannot exist either. When all dust motes are gone, then not even one dust mote exists.

All dharmas (phenomena) have no intrinsic substance, nothing to depend on. They arise expediently through a false process of combination.

Some people say that everything in the universe is invisibly controlled by a Lord. Most religions say that there is a Creator who creates the myriad things, and that everything in the world is created by him. In reality, no one can be the lord of the myriad things. There is no creator and nothing that is created.

How do we explain things, then? We can explain everything in terms of becoming deluded, committing offenses, and undergoing retribution. Where does karma come from? It comes from deluded thinking. Initially there is non-enlightenment, or ignorance. Ignorance gives rise to confusion. Without ignorance, confusion would not arise. When there is confusion, we engage in deluded thinking, and then create all kinds of karma.

造的業，是善因，就有善的果報；是惡因，就有惡的果報；是不善不惡因，就有不善不惡的果報。

所以眾生所遭所遇，無非是自己所造的，並不是其他人所造、所支配的，一切都是自己。乃至在輪迴中轉來轉去，不能出離，隨業而受果報，生生死死，死死生生，永不離開生死，都是自己所造的。怎能知道是這樣呢？因為要是離開這種道理，就沒有其他道理可講了。

有的宗教主張世間一切是受神的支配；既然是受神的支配，那麼造善造惡與自己就沒有關係。但是到時候受果報，還是要自己去受，神幫不了忙，可見這是不合理的道理。因為這個緣故，所以說果報是從自己的業感召而生出來的，正所謂「如是因，如是果。」

好像有人主使別人去殺人，這人雖然犯罪，可是主使人也有罪；如果神來支配我們，一切一切都由神來作主，那麼我們所造的業，神應該分一半果報，

If we create good karma, we receive a pleasant retribution. With evil karma, we undergo an unpleasant retribution. If the karma is neither good nor evil, the retribution will also be neutral.

Everything that happens to us is a result of the karma we created ourselves; we are not controlled or created by anyone else. We go round and round on the wheel of rebirth, receiving retributions according to our karma, never managing to escape from birth and death. This is also our own doing. How do we know? There is no other logical explanation of the matter.

Some religions say that everything in this world is controlled by God. If that were true, it wouldn't matter whether we did good or evil. But the reality is that, when the time comes, we ourselves have to undergo the retribution for our own deeds and God cannot help us. Therefore it's not sensible to say that God controls everything. Rather, we bring the reward or retribution upon ourselves through what we do. "As you sow, so shall you reap."

If one person tells another to commit murder, the first person is also guilty. By the same principle, if we are controlled by God, then it is only reasonable that God share half of our karmic retribution. We simply did what God told us to do, so we shouldn't have to suffer the consequences alone—it wouldn't be fair!

才合情理。如果不是這樣，神教我們所作的事情，罪全歸我們受，這就不平等、不合理了！

我們自己所造的業，與他人無關，我們所作的是善事，就得善的果報；所作的是惡事，就得惡的果報，這是很合理的因果。所以我們一舉一動，並不受任何人或神來支配。如果眞是受神支配的話，那神就不應該教我們做種種惡，應該只教我們做種種善，這樣才對。因爲神不願意人做惡事，希望人做善事。如果神沒有這個能力，那麼我們做惡，還是自己受報，做功德是祂的，做惡是我們自己承擔的，這太不合邏輯學了。

一九八〇年六月二十日開示

Actually, the offenses we commit have nothing to do with anyone else. If we do good deeds, we receive good results; evil deeds reap bad results. This principle of cause and effect is very reasonable. We are not controlled by any person or any god in what we do. If we were ruled by a god, he should keep us from doing evil and cause us to do good. Gods and spirits like to see people do good and refrain from evil. But since they don't have the power to control us, we must still take the retribution for our evil deeds. For them to take the credit for our meritorious acts, while we bear the consequences for our evil deeds, is totally illogical!

A talk given on June 20, 1980

把心的開關打開

自己的智慧光明現出來，就是佛光普照。

佛光普照，佛的智慧光明，普照一切眾生心，把眾生的心照亮了，把貪瞋癡消滅除盡，把黑暗照成光明，息滅眾生八萬四千種的習氣毛病。我們學佛法，就是要滅除貪瞋癡，不要執著。

你說：「我怎麼沒看見佛呢？」

研究佛法，開了智慧，這豈不是佛光嗎？若越研究越糊塗，不懂真正佛法的道理，是因爲自己沒有滅除習氣毛病，不能說佛光不普照。自己不開智慧，貪瞋癡還是老樣子，一點也沒有改，那佛光普照，

Flipping on the Switch in Our Mind

When the light of your wisdom appears, just that is the Buddha's light shining everywhere.

The Buddha's light shines everywhere. The light of the Buddha's wisdom illumines all living beings' minds, purging them of greed, hatred, and delusion. That light dispels the darkness and eradicates 84,000 bad habits and faults. We are studying Buddhism because we want to get rid of greed, hatred, and delusion, and cast off our attachments.

"Why haven't I seen the Buddha's light?" you ask.

Isn't studying the Buddha's teachings and uncovering our wisdom seeing the Buddha's light? If you don't understand the teachings and studying them only makes you more confused, it's because you haven't renounced your bad habits and faults. You can't say that the Buddha's light doesn't shine everywhere. If you don't develop your wisdom and hang on to your greed, hatred, and delusion, then

也非所照。不是有照，也不是無照，是照而不照，無照而照。這就是說，自己的智慧光明現出來，就是佛光普照；自己的智慧光明不現出來，就是佛光不普照。

佛光譬如電力公司，在我們所住的房子裏，將電線、電燈的開關等等，都已裝妥，接通電力了。但是如果不去按開關，這電燈始終不會明亮，這屋內也永遠是黑暗的。爲什麼？因爲電不通，不起作用。若按開關，立刻燈光明亮，照破黑暗。我們眾生的心，就是開關，把心的開關打開，佛光就亮了。若心的開關不開，就是有佛光，也照不到。這個譬喻雖淺，但有相同之理。各位！快把心的開關打開，接受佛的智慧光來引證，這樣就得到佛光普照。

一九八〇年七月四日開

even though the Buddha's light shines everywhere, it can't shine on you. It neither shines nor doesn't shine; it shines without shining. When the light of your wisdom appears, just that is the Buddha's light shining everywhere. Before your own wisdom light has come forth, for you the Buddha's light doesn't shine everywhere.

The Buddha's light is like the electricity from the power company. The cables and switches may be installed in the house, but if we don't switch on the lights, the house will remain dark. Why? Because the power isn't connected. As soon as we flip on the switch, the lights go on and the darkness is gone. Our mind can be compared to a light switch. If we turn on the switch in our mind, the Buddha's light will shine forth. If we can't flip the switch, then even though the Buddha's light is there, it can't connect. This is a simple analogy, but it conveys the principle. Everyone should quickly turn on the switch in his or her mind and receive the guidance of the Buddha's wisdom light. That's what it means to be illumined by the Buddha's universal light.

A talk given on July 4, 1980

開悟的鑰匙

在你心中有一把鎖，
一定要有一把鑰匙，才能把鎖打開。

人怎樣才能開悟呢？開悟好像開鎖一樣。鎖能把門鎖上，禁止你出入，你一定要有一把鑰匙，才能把門鎖打開；否則將永遠被禁在屋中。那麼這把鑰匙放在那裏？就在你自己的身邊，很容易找到。怎樣去找呢？你現在參禪打坐、念佛、持咒，就是在找鑰匙。什麼時候能找到呢？就要看你自己的修行程度而定。如果精進，很快就找到；如果懈怠，就永遠找不到，不但今生找不到，即使來生也找不到。這種道理非常簡單。

在你心中也有一把鎖，這把心鎖就是無明，它能使

228

The Key to Enlightenment

There is a locked door in your mind, and you have to use a key to unlock it.

How can we become enlightened? Enlightenment can be compared to unlocking a door. When the door is locked, you can't go in or out through it. You have to use a key to unlock the door. If you don't have the key, then you'll be locked inside the house forever. Where is the key? It's right where you are; it's very easy to find. How can you find it? As you sit in Chan meditation, recite the Buddha's name, and recite mantras, you are looking for the key. When will you find it? It depends on the level of your cultivation. If you are vigorous, you will find the key very quickly. If you are lax, you'll never find it, not in this life or in lives to come. This is a very simple principle.

In the analogy, the lock in your mind represents the ignorance that causes your pure and bright mind to become dark and defiled. When you encounter situations, if you

你清淨光明的心，變成染污黑暗的心。境界來了，沒有智慧去判別是善是惡，便做出顛倒事。你修行得力，便能把無明破了。藉著鑰匙，心鎖自然打開，智慧光明現出之後，無論遇到什麼事，也都沒有煩惱了。

什麼是無明？簡而言之，就是黑暗，什麼都不明白。因爲不明白眞理，把心鎖上了，所以不能開悟。

在唐朝代宗皇帝時，有個太監，名叫魚朝恩，他問國師：「什麼是無明？」國師說：「你這副奴才相，那有資格問佛法？」他勃然大怒。國師笑說：「這就是無明。」所謂「無明火能燒功德林。」

現在能夠開悟的人，都是在從前修種種善因，今生才成就。如果以前沒有修種種善因，今生不會開悟。想要開悟？一定要預先修行，才有開悟的希望。

釋迦牟尼佛，他怎能在今生成佛呢？因爲他

　　　三祇修福慧，
　　　百劫種相好。

lack the wisdom to distinguish good from evil, you will act in deluded ways. After you have gained skill in your practice, you will be able to smash through ignorance and unlock the door of your mind to reveal bright wisdom. Then no matter what happens, you won't get afflicted.

What is ignorance? To put it simply, it is darkness, or lack of understanding. When we don't understand the truth, our mind is locked up and we cannot attain enlightenment. During the reign of Emperor Taizong of the Tang dynasty, there was a eunuch named Yu Chao'en. Yu Chao'en asked the National Master [the Dharma Master who was the emperor's spiritual teacher], "What is ignorance?"

The National Master said, "You look like a slave. What makes you think you're qualified to ask about the Buddhadharma?" The eunuch was furious. The National Master smiled and said, "That is ignorance." A proverb says: "The fire of ignorance can burn up a forest of merit and virtue."

People are able to become enlightened only because they cultivated many good deeds in their past lives. If they hadn't cultivated those good deeds, they wouldn't attain enlightenment in this life. Do you want to become enlightened? Then you must first cultivate. Only then will there be hope for enlightenment.

How did Shakyamuni Buddha achieve Buddhahood?

> He cultivated blessings and wisdom
> for three *asamkhyeya kalpas*.
> And planted the causes for the fine hallmarks
> for a hundred eons.

三大阿僧祇劫中修福又修慧，又在一百個大劫中修三十二相、八十種好的功德，因此他在菩提樹下，夜睹明星而悟道。如果他以前沒有修行，今生便不會成佛。

一九八〇年七月十二日開示

For three great *asamkhyeya kalpas* (uncountable eons), he cultivated blessings and wisdom. For a hundred great eons, he performed merit that led to his being adorned with the Thirty-two Hallmarks and Eighty Subsidiary Characteristics. That's why he was able to become enlightened upon seeing a bright star one night while sitting under the Bodhi tree. If he hadn't cultivated in the past, he couldn't have achieved Buddhahood when he did.

A talk given on July 12,1980

念佛是誰

有所執著，就是人心；
無有執著，就是道心。

現在是討論問題的時間，誰有問題就提出來，讓大
家研究研究。有人提出「念佛是誰」的問題。《金
剛經》上說：「應無所住而生其心」，若有一個地
方，那就是「住」；無所住就是不思善、不思惡，
就在這個地方上用功。要是注意在一個地方，想好
、想不好，這都是執著。修行就是修無所執著；什
麼執著都沒有了，把自己的身體也忘了。連身體都
沒有了，還有什麼執著呢？

在打坐參禪時，什麼都不念，只念「念佛是誰？」
念佛是哪一個？就找這個「誰」。什麼時候找到「

Who Is Mindful of the Buddha?

It is human nature to be attached. Freedom from attachments is the Way.

Now is the time for questions and answers. Whoever has questions can bring them up, and we can all investigate them together. Someone raised the question of "Who is mindful of the Buddha?" The *Vajra Sutra* says, "One should produce the mind which dwells nowhere." If there is a place, there is still dwelling. Dwelling nowhere means thinking of neither good nor evil. This is where we should focus our effort. If we pay attention to the place, thinking of it as good or bad, these are all attachments. We practice in order to be free from attachments. We want to get rid of all attachments and forget even our bodies. Without a body, how could we still have attachments?

When we sit in meditation, we shouldn't think of anything but the question: "Who is mindful of the Buddha?" Who is the one being mindful of the Buddha? Look for the "who."

誰」，什麼時候就開悟。找不到，一天要找，十天要找，百天要找，千天要找，萬天要找。一年十年百年千年萬年，都是在找這個；什麼時候找到，什麼時候才了。

不能想快，不是像吸鴉片菸，吸完就過癮了，沒有那麼容易的事情，那是騙人的法門。修真正的法門，要自己努力用功，不要有揠苗助長的思想：「快點長大吧！快點長高吧！」這是錯誤的思想。

「念佛是誰？」能把一切妄念都斬斷了，一切欲念都斬斷了，也就是斬盡十大魔軍。這個「誰」字，就是金剛王寶劍，什麼都斬乾淨，什麼都沒有了。並不是執著哪一個地方，「凡所有相，皆是虛妄，若見諸相非相，即見如來。」有所執著，就是人心；無有執著，就是道心。打坐不參這個「誰」字，妄想就生出來，這樣不會開悟。參話頭就是以毒攻毒，用妄想來控制妄想，也就是用一個妄想去調伏多個妄想，到了山窮水盡無路可走時，轉身處便是開悟時。

一九八〇年九月九日開示

When you find out "who" it is, you will be enlightened. If you can't find it, you must keep searching for one day, ten days, a hundred, a thousand days, ten thousand days! You continue searching for one year, ten, a hundred, a thousand, or ten thousand years, not stopping until you find it.

You cannot speed up the process. It's not like taking drugs and getting an immediate high. It's not that easy. Any "easy" practice is just a gimmick. A real method of practice requires hard work. Don't be like the farmer who tried to help his crops grow faster by pulling the shoots upwards. That's a mistake.

Contemplating "Who is mindful of Buddha?" can cut through all random thoughts and desires. This one thought destroys ten great demon armies. The word "who" is like a jeweled *vajra* sword that slashes through everything until there are no further attachments. "All appearances are false and illusory. If one sees all appearances as nonappearances, one sees the Thus Come One." It is human nature to be attached. Freedom from attachments is the Way. If we don't look into the question of "who" as we sit in meditation, random thoughts will arise and hinder our enlightenment. Investigating the question is a way of fighting fire with fire, focusing on one thought to subdue other random thoughts. When we reach a point in our investigation where we can neither go forward nor turn back, right then we'll become enlightened.

A talk given on September 9, 1980

附錄
APPENDICES

辭彙解釋
GLOSSARY

索引
INDEX

法界佛教總會簡介
THE DHARMA REALM BUDDHIST ASSOCIATION

宣化上人簡傳
A BIOGRAPHICAL SKETCH OF THE VENERABLE MASTER HSUAN HUA

宣化上人十八大願
THE EIGHTEEN GREAT VOWS OF THE VENERABLE MASTER HSUAN HUA

宇宙白
WHITE UNIVERSE

Glossary

This glossary is to aid readers unfamiliar with the Buddhist vocabulary. Definitions have been kept simple, and are not necessarily complete.

Ananda, Venerable 阿難尊者 One of the ten great disciples of the Buddha Shakyamuni, Ananda was the Buddha's first cousin and his attendant. He also compiled and edited the Sutras, and was the Second Patriarch in India.

Arhat 阿羅漢 An enlightened sage of the Small Vehicle. There are four stages of Arhatship.

1. The Arhat of the first stage is called a 'stream-enterer' (Srotaapanna). He has entered the stream of the Dharma-nature of the sage, and he goes counter to the flow of the stream of the six senses of common people. He still has to undergo seven more rebirths in the heavens and among humans before he comes to the end of the Path.

2. The Arhat of the second stage is called a 'once-returner' (Sakridagamin). He has one more birth to undergo in the heavens and one among humans.

3. The Arhat of the third stage is called a 'never-returner' (Anagamin). He does not have to undergo birth again in the human realm.

4. The Arhat of the fourth stage is called 'unborn.' The fourth stage Arhat has attained patience with the nonarising of dharmas.

asamkhyeya 阿僧祇 One of the large numbers used in ancient India, *asamkhyeya* translates as "uncountable."

asuras 阿修羅 A Sanskrit term interpreted as "beings who like to fight," *asuras* are one of the eightfold division of ghosts and spirits. *Asuras* are found in the heavens, human realm, and among animals and ghosts.

Avatamsaka Sutra 華嚴經 The *Avatamsaka Sutra* (*Flower Adornment Sutra*), the King of Kings among Sutras, was the first Sutra spoken after the Buddha became enlightened, and describes the practice of the Bodhisattva Path.

birth and death 生死 The state of common, unenlightened beings, who perceive themselves as being born and dying, transmigrating endlessly in the six paths of rebirth.

Bodhi resolve 菩提心 (In Sanskrit, *bodhicitta*.) The resolve to achieve Bodhi (enlightenment) through spiritual practice. Also translated as Bodhi mind.

Bodhisattva 菩薩 An enlightened being who does not enter Nirvana but chooses instead to remain in the world and save living beings.

Bodhisattva Path 菩薩道 The path followed by those who bring forth the Bodhi resolve. The cultivation of the six *paramitas* (giving, holding precepts, patience, vigor, samadhi, and wisdom) and the myriad practices is an essential aspect of the Bodhisattva Path.

Book of Rites 禮記 One of the Five Classics (see entry) of Confucianism, it contains the "Essay on the Achievement of Universal Harmony, Equality, and Justice through the Use of Propriety" describing the ideal society envisioned by Confucius.

Brahma Net Sutra 梵網經 Originally part of a much larger scripture called the *Bodhisattva Precepts Sutra*, this Sutra contains the Ten Major and Forty-eight Minor Bodhisattva Precepts.

Buddha 佛 One who has achieved the ultimate, perfect enlightenment.

Buddhadharma 佛法 The methods of cultivation taught by the Buddha that lead beings to enlightenment.

Buddha nature 佛性 The potential for Buddhahood that is inherent in all living beings. The Buddha-nature is nondual and all beings are equally endowed with it. It does not increase in an enlightened being nor is it less in a confused being.

Chan 禪 The abbreviated Chinese transliteration of the Sanskrit word *dhyana*. The general meaning of *dhyana* is meditation. The Japanese pronounce the character *chan* as 'Zen.' The Chan School is foremost among the Five Great Schools of Buddhism in that it transmits the Buddha's Mind Seal, pointing directly to the mind so that one sees one's nature and becomes a Buddha.

241

Confucius 孔子 The foremost sage and philosopher of China who lived in the fifth century B.C., he taught that every person should fulfill his or her proper role in family and society. His philosophy forms the basis of Chinese culture and tradition.

Confucianism 儒教 The teachings of Confucius, which stress the fulfillment of moral obligations and the development of virtue.

cultivation 修行 The practical application of the methods taught by the Buddha that lead to enlightenment. Such spiritual practice is likened to the process of cultivating a field, starting from plowing and planting and resulting in fruition, harvest, and storage.

delusion in thoughts 思惑 Defined as "giving rise to discriminations because one is confused about principles." There are eighty-one categories of delusion in thoughts.

delusion in views 見惑 Defined as "giving rise to greed when confronted with things." There are eighty-eight categories of delusion in views.

demon 魔 From the Sanskrit *mara*, the term means "bringer of death."

dharma 法 (1) A generic term for all the various kinds of things or entities that exist in the world, including both physical and mental phenomena. (2) A method.

Dharma 佛法 (Also: Buddhadharma) The teachings of Buddhas.

Dharma body 法身 The embodiment of Truth; the spiritual or "true" body of the Buddha, which is universally pervasive.

Dharma assembly 法會 A gathering where the Dharma is expounded or practiced.

Dharma-door 法門 A method of practice.

Dharma-ending Age 末法時代 The last of the three ages of Dharma. After the Buddha speaks the Dharma, there follows the Proper Dharma Age, which lasts 1000 years. It is followed by the Dharma Image Age, which also lasts 1000 years. The last period is the Dharma-ending Age, the age strong in fighting, which lasts for 10,000 years. During this age, the understanding and practice of the Buddha's teachings gradually decline and finally disappear.

Dharma Flower Sutra 法華經 Also known as the *Lotus Sutra*, this is one of the most important Mahayana Sutras; spoken by the Buddha in the final stage of his teaching, it is the Sutra for the realization of Buddhahood.

Dharma Master 法師 A teacher of Dharma. A respectful term of address for members of the Sangha.

Dharma Realm 法界 (1) The enlightened world, the totality of the realm of the Buddhas. (2) A particular plane of existence, such as one of the ten Dharma Realms of Buddhist cosmology. There are four sagely Dharma Realms (those of Buddhas, Bodhisattvas, Pratyekabuddhas, and Hearers) and six common Dharma Realms (those of gods, *asuras*, humans, animals, hungry ghosts, and hell-beings).

Dharma-protecting spirits 護法神 Invisible beings who have resolved or made vows to protect the Buddha's teachings. These beings include the eightfold division of gods, dragons, *yakshas* ('speedy ghosts'), *gandharvas* (incense-inhaling spirits), *asuras* (beings who like to fight), *garudas* (great eagle-like birds), *kinnaras* (musical spirits), and *mahoragas* (great python-spirits).

Dhyana 禪 A Sanskrit word which translates as "stilling one's thoughts" and refers to meditation. *Chan* in Chinese, *zen* in Japanese.

Dhyana Master 禪師 A Buddhist monastic who specializes in meditation.

eighth consciousness 第八識 According to the Consciousness-only school, living beings possess eight distinct layers of consciousness, five associated with the sense faculties (eyes, ears, nose, tongue, body), the sixth with the thinking mind, the seventh with the sense of ego, and the eighth being the repository of all impressions from one's experiences. The eighth consciousness is the base from which the other seven arise.

false thoughts 妄想 The discursive thoughts of the conscious mind, which obstruct the wisdom of our inherent nature.

243

filiality 孝順 Also known as filial piety, it refers to respect and appreciation for parents, teachers, and elders.

Five Classics 五經 The five Confucian classical texts: The *Yijing (Book of Changes)*, the *Book of History*, the *Book of Rites*, the *Book of Odes*, and the *Spring and Autumn Annals*.

five desires 五欲 The desires for wealth, sex, fame, food, and sleep. These desires are the "roots of the hells."

Five Eyes 五眼 These five spiritual eyes, possessed by all people, will open in the process of diligent cultivation. They are the Buddha Eye, the Wisdom Eye, the Dharma Eye, the Heavenly Eye, and the Flesh Eye.

Five Precepts 五戒 The fundamental precepts received by laity, they are: no killing, no stealing, no sexual misconduct, no lying, and no intoxicants (including cigarettes and drugs of all kinds).

Flower Adornment Sutra 華嚴經 See *Avatamsaka Sutra*.

Four Books 四書 The four basic Confucian texts: *The Analects*, *The Great Learning*, *The Doctrine of the Mean*, and *The Book of Mencius*.

Four Noble Truths 四聖諦 The Buddha's teachings for the Arhat disciples, they are (1) the Truth of Suffering, (2) the Truth of Accumulation, (3) the Truth of Extinction, and (4) the Truth of the Way.

gods 天神 Gods, according to Buddhist teaching, live in various heavens. They are not immortal or omnipotent. They do have long life spans and various spiritual powers. Anyone can be reborn as a god by generating the appropriate good karma; however, gods are not enlightened. They eventually die and are reborn in lower realms according to their karma.

golden-winged *peng* birds 大鵬金翅鳥 Also known as *garudas*, they have a wingspan of about 3000 miles.

Guanyin (Guanshiyin) Bodhisattva 觀音菩薩 (In Sanskrit, Avalokiteshvara Bodhisattva.) Of the four great Bodhisattvas who have affinities with our world, Guanyin is the Bodhisattva of Great Compassion. His name means "Contemplating the Sounds of the World."

244

Hearers 聲聞 Also known as Arhats, these are the Buddha's disciples who awaken to the Way by hearing the sound of the Buddha's teachings.

inherent nature 自性 Another name for the Buddha nature inherent in all living beings.

karma 業 A Sanskrit word that means "deeds," what we do. Karma can be good, evil, or neutral and is created by body, mouth, and mind.

King Yama 閻羅王 There are ten King Yamas in Jambudvipa who rule over ghosts, and send the Ghost of Impermanence to give human beings notice when their time of death is at hand. After death, in the Courts of the King Yamas, offenses are judged and rewards and retributions determined. King Yama has a stern appearance and an uncompromising attitude, but the heart of a Bodhisattva.

Land of Ultimate Bliss 極樂世界 (In Sanskrit, Sukhavati.) The Buddhaland of Amitabha Buddha in the West created through the power of his 48 vows which enable living beings to be reborn in his land simply by sincere mindfulness and recitation of his name. Also known as the Western Pure Land.

leave the home life 出家 To renounce the life of a householder and enter the Sangha (Buddhist monastic order).

left-home people 出家人 A generic term for Buddhist monks and nuns.

mantra 咒 Mantras are phrases of sound whose primary meanings are not cognitive, but on a spiritual level that transcends ordinary linguistic understanding.

Mount Sumeru 須彌山 The Sanskrit word Sumeru means "Wonderfully High." It is the central mountain of every world-system.

Nirvana 涅槃 A state of ultimate tranquility, perfect quiescence realized by enlightened sages.

patience with the nonarising of dharmas 無生法忍 At the Fourth Stage of Arhatship, one awakens to the patience with the nonarising of dharmas; within the universe, one sees not the slightest dharma produced nor the slightest dharma destroyed. This ineffable state cannot be expressed, but can only be endured in the heart.

prajna 般若 *Prajna* is transcendental wisdom. The word is left in Sanskrit because it has many meanings and the English word "wisdom" doesn't cover them all. There are: (1) literary *prajna*, (2) contemplative *prajna*, and (3) the *prajna* of reality.

Pratyekabuddhas (Those Enlightened by Conditions) 辟支佛 （緣覺） Those who attain enlightenment through contemplating the Twelve Causal Conditions (see entry).

precepts 戒律 Rules of ethical conduct set forth by the Buddha to help cultivators regulate their bodies, mouths, and minds. In Buddhism, there are 5 precepts for laypeople, 10 precepts for novices, 250 precepts for fully ordained monks and 348 precepts for fully-ordained nuns, and 10 major and 48 minor Bodhisattva precepts for those who bring forth the Bodhisattva resolve.

Pure Land 淨土 Normally used as another name for the Western Land of Ultimate Bliss, this term can also apply to any Buddha's pure land.

samadhi 定 Concentration attained through meditation and other practices. There are many types and levels of samadhi. Precepts are the basis for developing samadhi, and samadhi leads to wisdom.

Sangha 僧伽 The order of Buddhist monks and nuns.

Sanskrit 梵文 An ancient Indian language belonging to the Indic branch of the Indo-European family of languages; the language in which the Mahayana Buddhist Sutras were preserved.

Shakyamuni Buddha 釋迦牟尼佛 The historical Buddha of this world who was born in India as Prince Siddhartha Gautama over 2500 years ago.

Shastras 論 Commentaries on the teachings of the Buddha spoken by Buddhist Patriarchs and disciples of the Buddha.

Shurangama Mantra 楞嚴咒 The longest and most powerful mantra in Buddhism, contained within the *Shurangama Sutra*.

Shurangama Sutra 楞嚴經 One of the most important Mahayana Sutras in Buddhism, it will be the first Sutra to disappear in the Dharma-ending Age.

six paths of rebirth 六道輪迴 The realms where common, unenlightened beings revolve within the cycle of birth and death. These realms are those of gods, *asuras*, humans, animals, hungry ghosts, and hell-beings.

Six Perfections 六度 The practices of Bodhisattvas, also called the six *paramitas*, they are: giving, holding precepts, patience, vigor, samadhi, and wisdom.

spiritual penetrations 神通 There are six spiritual penetrations: (1) the heavenly eye, (2) the heavenly ear, (3) the knowledge of others' thoughts, (4) the knowledge of past lives, (5) the complete spirit, and (6) the ending of outflows. These supernatural powers come naturally as a part of cultivation, but are not the goal of cultivation. Gods, spirits, and ghosts have attained only the first five in varying degrees.

Sun, Yatsen 孫中山 A Chinese statesman who lived 1866–1925, Dr. Sun was the father of the modern Republic of China (Taiwan).

Sutras 經 Buddhist scriptures that consist of discourses spoken by Buddhas, Bodhisattvas, or other enlightened disciples of the Buddhas.

Tao, Yuanming 陶淵明 372-427 A.D. A classical Chinese poet of the Jin dynasty, he resigned from his governmental post and retired to the countryside. His poems are filled with nature scenes and descriptions of simple farming life.

Taoism 道教 A Chinese mystical philosophy founded by the sage Lao Zi in the sixth century B.C. that teaches conformity to the Tao by unassertive action and simplicity.

Tathagata 如來 One of the ten titles that a Buddha has, the Sanskrit word "Tathagata" may be translated as "Thus Come One".

Ten Dharma Realms 十法界 The Ten Dharma Realms are divided into Four Realms of the Sages (Buddhas, Bodhisattvas, Those Enlightened to Conditions, and Hearers) and Six paths of rebirth (gods, humans, *asuras*, animals, hungry ghosts, and hell-beings).

Ten Good Deeds 十善 There are three of the body: no killing, no stealing, no sexual misconduct; three of the mind: no greed, no anger, no delusion; and four of the mouth: no harsh speech, no backbiting, no lying, and no loose speech.

Thirty-seven Limbs of Enlightenment 三十七菩提道品 These are thirty-seven kinds of practices for the attainment of enlightenment. They are: the Four Applications of Mindfulness, the Four Right Efforts, the Four Bases of Psychic Powers, the Five Roots, the Five Powers, the Seven Limbs of Enlightenment, and the Eightfold Holy Path.

Thirty-two Hallmarks and Eighty Subsidiary Characteristics 三十二相八十隨形好 Hallmarks of all Buddhas, extending from the crowns of their heads to the soles of their feet, achieved through the perfection of blessings and wisdom.

three evil paths 三惡道 The paths/destinies of animals, hungry ghosts, and hell-beings are said to be evil, since they entail much more suffering than the good paths of gods, *asuras*, and humans.

Three Realms 三界 The Desire Realm, in which we live; the Form Realm, heavens free of desire that are reached through meditation and cultivation; and the Formless Realm; heavens free of desire and form that are reached through meditation and cultivation.

Three Refuges 三皈依 The formulas for taking refuge in the Triple Jewel—the Buddha, the Dharma, and the Sangha.

Thus Come One 如來 (In Sanskrit, Tathagata.) One of the ten titles of a Buddha.

Tripitaka ("Three Treasuries") 三藏 The Buddhist Canon, which is divided into three divisions—Sutras, Vinaya, and Shastras.

Triple Jewel 三寶 Also called the Three Jewels or Gems, it comprises: (1) the Buddha, (2) the Dharma, and (3) the Sangha. They are Buddhism's greatest treasures. For further information, see the individual entries for each.

Triple Realm 三界 See Three Realms above.

Twelve Causal Conditions 十二因緣 Those Enlightened to Conditions (Pratyekabuddhas) become enlightened by contemplating both the arising and the cessation of these twelve, which condition each other in the following sequence:

1. ignorance is the condition for activity;
2. activity is the condition for consciousness;

3. consciousness is the condition for name and form;
4. name and form are the condition for the six sense faculties;
5. the six sense faculties are the condition for contact;
6. contact is the condition for feeling;
7. feeling is the condition for emotional love;
8. emotional love is the condition for grasping;
9. grasping is the condition for becoming;
10. becoming is the condition for birth;
11. birth is the condition for
12. old age and death.

vajra 金剛 An indestructible substance that is usually represented by diamond, the Sanskrit name means "durable," "luminous," and "able to cut."

Universal Door Chapter 普門品 The twenty-fifth chapter in the *Dharma Flower Sutra*. It describes the spiritual powers of Guanyin Bodhisattva and the responses gained from praying to that Bodhisattva.

Vajra (Diamond) Sutra 金剛經 One of the most popular Buddhist Sutras, the *Vajra Prajna Paramita Sutra* explains how the Bodhisattva relies on the perfection of wisdom to teach and transform beings.

Vinaya 戒律 The collected moral regulations governing the life of the Buddhist monastic community, one of the three divisions of the Buddhist canon. The Vinaya includes all the precept-regulations, methods we use to keep watch over ourselves so that it is not necessary for anyone else to keep an eye on us.

Way (Tao) 道 The spiritual path of cultivation; the ultimate truth, which is realized through following that path.

Way-place 道場 (In Sanskrit, Bodhimanda.) (1) A "site of enlightenment." (2) Any place of practice—a temple, a monastery, a hermitage—regardless of its size.

World Honored One 世尊 One of the ten titles of all Buddhas. Buddhas are honored both in and beyond the world.

Index

A

B

Index of First Lines of Poems

法界佛教總會簡介

宗旨

法界佛教總會，前身爲中美佛教總會，創辦人——
上宣下化老和尚一九五九年創立於美國。本會以法界
爲體，以將佛教的眞實義理，普遍傳播到世界各地
；以翻譯經典、弘揚正法、提倡道德教育、利樂有
情爲己任。俾使個人、家庭、社會、國家，乃至世
界，皆能蒙受佛法的薰習，而漸趨至眞、至善、至
美的境地。

創辦人簡介

上人，名安慈，字度輪，接虛雲老和尚法，嗣潙仰
，法號宣化。籍東北，誕於清末民初。年十九出家
，廬墓守孝。修禪定，習教觀，日一食，夜不臥。
一九四八年抵香港，成立佛教講堂等道場。一九六
二年攜正法西來，在美開演大乘經典數十部。歷年
來，除建立法界佛教總會及所隸屬萬佛聖城等正法
道場二十多處外，並創辦譯經、教育等機構，法化

258

The Dharma Realm
Buddhist Association

Mission

The Dharma Realm Buddhist Association (formerly the Sino-American Buddhist Association) was founded by the Venerable Master Hsuan Hua in the United States of America in 1959. Taking the Dharma Realm as its scope, the Association aims to disseminate the genuine teachings of the Buddha throughout the world. The Association is dedicated to translating the Buddhist canon, propagating the Orthodox Dharma, promoting ethical education, and bringing benefit and happiness to all beings. Its hope is that individuals, families, the society, the nation, and the entire world will, under the transforming influence of the Buddhadharma, gradually reach the state of ultimate truth and goodness.

The Founder

The Venerable Master, whose names were An Tse and To Lun, received the Dharma name Hsuan Hua and the transmission of Dharma from Venerable Master Hsu Yun in the lineage of the Wei Yang Sect. He was born in Manchuria, China, at the beginning of the century. At nineteen, he entered the monastic order and dwelt in a hut by his mother's grave to practice filial piety. He meditated, studied the teachings, ate only one meal a day, and slept sitting up. In 1948 he went to Hong Kong, where he established the Buddhist Lecture Hall and other Way-places. In 1962 he brought the Proper Dharma to the West, lecturing on several dozen Mahayana Sutras in the United States. Over the years, the Master established more than twenty monasteries of Proper Dharma under the auspices of the Dharma Realm

東西方。一九九五年，上人示寂於美，而其一生大公無私，悲智雙運教化眾生的精神與德行，已感召無數人改過自新，走向清淨高尚的菩提大道。

弘法、譯經、教育

宣公上人一生之三大願：一、弘法。二、譯經。三、教育。為實現此三大願，上人本著三大宗旨、六大條款，不畏一切艱辛困苦，在西方建立道場，接引眾生，廣行教化。數十年來創辦的機構如下：

萬佛聖城、分支道場

為了弘揚正法，上人除了培育訓練人才之外，更致力於道場的建立，以期轉法輪，度眾生，提供修行人遵循佛制的清淨修持道場。歷年來分別成立正法道場多處，美加地區計有萬佛聖城、金山聖寺、金聖寺、金輪聖寺、金峰聖寺、金佛聖寺、華嚴聖寺、長堤聖寺、法界聖城、柏克萊寺、華嚴精舍、福祿壽聖寺等；臺灣地區則有法界佛教印經會、法界聖寺、彌陀聖寺；馬來西亞地區為紫雲洞、登彼岸

Buddhist Association and the City of Ten Thousand Buddhas. He also founded centers for the translation of the Buddhist canon and for education to spread the influence of the Dharma in the East and West. The Master manifested the stillness in the United States in 1995. Through his lifelong, selfless dedication to teaching living beings with wisdom and compassion, he influenced countless people to change their faults and to walk upon the pure, bright path to enlightenment.

Dharma Propagation, Buddhist Text Translation, and Education

The Venerable Master Hua's three great vows after leaving the home-life were (1) to propagate the Dharma, (2) to translate the Buddhist Canon, and (3) to promote education. In order to make these vows a reality, the Venerable Master based himself on the Three Principles and the Six Guidelines. Courageously facing every hardship, he founded monasteries, schools, and centers in the West, drawing in living beings and teaching them on a vast scale. Over the years, he founded the following institutions:

The City of Ten Thousand Buddhas and Its Branches

In propagating the Proper Dharma, the Venerable Master not only trained people but also founded Way-places where the Dharma wheel could turn and living beings could be saved. He wanted to provide cultivators with pure places to practice in accord with the Buddha's regulations. Over the years, he founded many Way-places of Proper Dharma. In the United States and Canada, these include the City of Ten Thousand Buddhas; Gold Mountain Monastery; Gold Sage Monastery; Gold Wheel Monastery; Gold Summit Monastery; Gold Buddha Monastery; Avatamsaka Monastery; Long Beach Monastery; the City of the Dharma Realm;

，蓮華精舍等道場；香港地區道場則是佛教講堂、慈興寺等。

萬佛聖城購於一九七四年，爲法界佛教總會樞紐，位於舊金山以北一百一十英哩的曼第仙諾縣達摩鎮內。佔地四百八十八英畝，已開闢使用的場地約八十英畝；其餘爲草原、果園及樹林。城中有七十餘座大型建築物，大小房間二千餘間，清幽寧靜，空氣清新，是美國第一座大型的佛教道場，也是國際性的正法道場。

宣公上人雖爲禪宗潙仰派第九代傳人，但所屬道場一切作息、法會與修持，均兼顧禪、淨、密、律、教五宗的修持法門，一律平等重視，正契合佛陀所說的「是法平等，無有高下」。道場內清規嚴謹，住眾皆須嚴以律己，勤奮不懈，以正法爲依歸，過著清淨無染、大公無私、身心安樂的生活；日日講經說法，轉法輪，奉獻身心，爲復興佛教而努力。所有的道場除了遵守佛制：「日中一食、衣不離體」外，並遵守三大宗旨：

Berkeley Buddhist Monastery; Avatamsaka Hermitage; and Blessings, Prosperity, and Longevity Monastery. In Taiwan, there are the Dharma Realm Buddhist Books Distribution Association, Dharma Realm Monastery, and Amitabha Monastery. In Malaysia, there are Zi Yun Dong Monastery, Deng Bi An Monastery, and Lotus Vihara. In Hong Kong, there are the Buddhist Lecture Hall and Cixing Monastery.

Purchased in 1974, the City of Ten Thousand Buddhas is the hub of the Dharma Realm Buddhist Association. The City is located in Talmage, Mendocino County, California, 110 miles north of San Francisco. Eighty of the 488 acres of land are in active use. The remaining acreage consists of meadows, orchards, and woods. With over seventy large buildings containing over 2,000 rooms, blessed with serenity and fresh, clean air, it is the first large Buddhist monastic community in the United States. It is also an international center for the Proper Dharma.

Although the Venerable Master Hua was the Ninth Patriarch in the Weiyang Sect of the Chan School, the monasteries he founded emphasize all of the five main practices of Mahayana Buddhism (Chan meditation, Pure Land, esoteric, Vinaya (moral discipline), and doctrinal studies). This accords with the Buddha's words: "The Dharma is level and equal, with no high or low." At the City of Ten Thousand Buddhas, the rules of purity are rigorously observed. Residents of the City strive to regulate their own conduct and to cultivate with vigor. Taking refuge in the Proper Dharma, they lead pure and selfless lives, and attain peace in body and mind. The Sutras are expounded and the Dharma wheel is turned daily. Residents dedicate themselves wholeheartedly to making Buddhism flourish. Monks and nuns in all the monasteries take one meal a day, always wear their precept sash, and follow the Three Principles:

凍死不攀緣，

餓死不化緣，

窮死不求緣；

隨緣不變，不變隨緣，

抱定我們三大宗旨。

捨命為佛事，

造命為本事，

正命為僧事；

即事明理，明理即事，

推行祖師一脈心傳。

六大條款：不爭、不貪、不求、不自私、不自利、不打妄語。

國際譯經學院

上人發願將三藏十二部皆譯成西方文字語言，流通全世界。故於一九七三年，在三藩市成立國際譯經學院，翻譯佛經為英文及其他語言。該院於一九七七年，合併於法界佛教大學內，成為譯經學院。於一九九一年，上人於柏林根市購下一棟大樓，為國

Freezing, we do not scheme.
Starving, we do not beg.
Dying of poverty, we ask for nothing.
According with conditions, we do not change.
Not changing, we accord with conditions.
We adhere firmly to our three great principles.
We renounce our lives to do the Buddha's work.
We take the responsibility to mold our own destinies.
We rectify our lives to fulfill the Sanghan's role.
Encountering specific matters,
  we understand the principles.
Understanding the principles,
  we apply them in specific matters.
We carry on the single pulse of
  the Patriarchs' mind-transmission.

The monasteries also follow the Six Guidelines: not contending, not being greedy, not seeking, not being selfish, not pursuing personal advantage, and not lying.

International Translation Institute

The Venerable Master vowed to translate the Buddhist Canon (Tripitaka) into Western languages so that it would be widely accessible throughout the world. In 1973, he founded the International Translation Institute on Washington Street in San Francisco for the purpose of translating Buddhist scriptures into English and other languages. In 1977, the Institute was merged into Dharma Realm Buddhist University as the Institute for the Translation of Buddhist Texts. In 1991, the Venerable Master purchased a large building in Burlingame (south of San Francisco) and established the International Translation Institute there for the purpose of translating and publishing Buddhist texts. To date, in addition to publishing over one

際譯經學院永久院址，旨在翻譯經典及出版佛書。歷年來，除了已發行中文版佛經、佛書一百多冊外，另有英文版、法文版、西班牙文版、越南文版、日文版、中英版等百多冊譯本。

此外，錄音帶、錄影帶亦相續出版中。發行近卅年的金剛菩提海月刊，近幾年來更以中英雙語對照版方式刊出。譯經這項龐大艱鉅的工作，中國過去皆由國王、皇帝主辦、支持，今日上人鼓勵弟子們共同努力挑起此重責大任，藉著書籍及有聲的出版工作，運用語言文字，轉正法輪，作大佛事。凡一切有心參與此神聖工作者，均應謹守譯經學院的八項基本守則：

一、不得抱有個人的名利。
二、不得貢高我慢，必須以虔誠恭敬的態度
　　來工作。
三、不得自讚毀他。
四、不得自以為是，對他人作品吹毛求疵。
五、以佛心為己心。
六、運用擇法眼來辨別正確的道理。

hundred volumes of Buddhist texts in Chinese, the Association has published more than one hundred volumes of English, French, Spanish, Vietnamese, and Japanese translations of Buddhist texts, as well as bilingual (Chinese and English) editions. Audio and video tapes also continue to be produced. The monthly journal *Vajra Bodhi Sea,* which has been in circulation for nearly thirty years, has been published in bilingual (Chinese and English) format in recent years.

In the past, the difficult and vast mission of translating the Buddhist canon in China was sponsored and supported by the emperors and kings themselves. In our time, the Venerable Master encouraged his disciples to cooperatively shoulder this heavy responsibility, producing books and audio tapes and using the medium of language to turn the wheel of Proper Dharma and do the great work of the Buddha. All those who aspire to devote themselves to this work of sages should uphold the Eight Guidelines of the International Translation Institute:

1. One must free oneself from the motives of personal fame and profit.

2. One must cultivate a respectful and sincere attitude free from arrogance and conceit.

3. One must refrain from aggrandizing one's work and denigrating that of others.

4. One must not establish oneself as the standard of correctness and suppress the work of others with one's fault-finding.

5. One must take the Buddha-mind as one's own mind.

6. One must use the wisdom of Dharma-Selecting Vision to determine true principles.

七、懇請十方大德長老印證其翻譯。

八、作品在獲得印證之後，必須努力弘揚流
　　通經、律、論以及佛書，以光大佛教。

這是上人的大願，亦是所有從事譯經工作者努力邁
進的目標。

育良小學、培德中學、法界佛教大學

「教育，就是最根本的國防。」宣公上人鑑於要拯
救世界，當務之急便是辦好教育；因為想救世界，
就要改造人心，使之去惡向善。故於一九七四年，
成立育良小學；一九七六年，成立培德中學及法界
佛教大學。

在融入佛教精神的教育下，小學以「孝」，中學以
「忠」，大學則以「仁義」等道德為宗旨。育良小
學、培德中學的課程，融合現代、傳統及東西文化
的優點，注重道德、精神的薰習。旨在培育出品格
高尚的世界棟樑之才，以利益世界人類。學校採中
英雙語教育，男女分校。學生們在校除接受一般美
國中小學所必須學習的科目外，並有倫理課、打坐

7. One must request Virtuous Elders of the ten directions to certify one's translations.
8. One must endeavor to propagate the teachings by printing Sutras, Shastra texts, and Vinaya texts when the translations are certified as being correct.

These are the Venerable Master's vows, and participants in the work of translation should strive to realize them.

Instilling Goodness Elementary School, Developing Virtue Secondary School, Dharma Realm Buddhist University

"Education is the best national defense." The Venerable Master Hua saw clearly that in order to save the world, it is essential to promote good education. If we want to save the world, we have to bring about a complete change in people's minds and guide them to cast out unwholesomeness and to pursue goodness. To this end the Master founded Instilling Goodness Elementary School in 1974, and Developing Virtue Secondary School and Dharma Realm Buddhist University in 1976.

In an education embodying the spirit of Buddhism, the elementary school teaches students to be filial to parents, the secondary school teaches students to be good citizens, and the university teaches such virtues as humaneness and righteousness. Instilling Goodness Elementary School and Developing Virtue Secondary School combine the best of contemporary and traditional methods and of Western and Eastern cultures. They emphasize moral virtue and spiritual development, and aim to guide students to become good and capable citizens who will benefit humankind. The schools offer

課、佛學課等,以奠定學生良好的道德基礎,逐步引導學生認識自我、探索宇宙的眞理。除了萬佛聖城之外,各道場亦設有育良小學、培德中學分校(週日班),將孝道及倫理道德等教育,普遍推行於各地。

以正法爲教學主要内容的法界佛教大學,不僅傳授專業知識,更注重以倫理道德爲基礎,擴展至幫助所有人類、一切眾生回歸自性的研習。故法界大學提倡共同研究、自由交換理念的風氣,鼓勵學生修學各種經典,以不同的經驗及學習層面,推動主觀智能,來發揮經典的意趣妙理;同時注重實際修持,使佛法與生活融合爲一,滋養慧命,充實德行,從中造就出品行高潔、出類拔萃的優秀人才,以利益群生。

僧伽居士訓練班

有鑑於末法時代,東西方社會普遍缺乏眞實依佛制行持、戒律精嚴的道場,以及具眞知灼見的明眼善知識,來引導有意從事佛教事業的人士。又爲了提高僧眾素質,令正法久住,造就行解並進的國際佛

a bilingual (Chinese/English) program where boys and girls study separately. In addition to standard academic courses, the curriculum includes ethics, meditation, Buddhist studies, and so on, giving students a foundation in virtue and guiding them to understand themselves and explore the truths of the universe. Branches of the schools (Sunday schools) have been established at branch monasteries with the aim of propagating filial piety and ethical education.

Dharma Realm Buddhist University, whose curriculum focuses on the Proper Dharma, does not merely transmit academic knowledge. It emphasizes a foundation in virtue, which expands into the study of how to help all living beings discover their inherent nature. Thus, Dharma Realm Buddhist University advocates a spirit of shared inquiry and free exchange of ideas, encouraging students to study various canonical texts and use different experiences and learning styles to tap their inherent wisdom and fathom the meanings of those texts. Students are encouraged to practice the principles they have understood and apply the Buddhadharma in their lives, thereby nurturing their wisdom and virtue. The University aims to produce outstanding individuals of high moral character who will be able to bring benefit to all sentient beings.

Sangha and Laity Training Programs
In the Dharma-ending Age, in both Eastern and Western societies there are very few monasteries that actually practice the Buddha's regulations and strictly uphold the precepts. Teachers with genuine wisdom and understanding, capable of guiding those who aspire to pursue careers in Buddhism, are very rare. The Venerable Master founded the Sangha and Laity Training Programs in 1982 with the goals of raising the caliber of the Sangha, perpetuating the Proper Dharma, providing

教人才，以續佛慧命。因此，上人於一九八二年成立僧伽居士訓練班。

僧伽訓練班為令出家眾在佛學修習方面，能奠定良好穩固的基礎，不但訓練僧眾實際參與佛教事務，建立僧團職事概念，以期畢業後，在各道場、寺廟，及其他環境中，擔任佛教的種種職務。又特別注重學生們充實佛教教理，深入經藏；認真修行，嚴持戒律，培養高尚德行，以弘揚正法，續佛慧命。居士訓練班亦予居士適當的課程，使學生們具正知正見，修持佛法、研究教理，齊頭並進，了解寺院的種種規矩與禮儀，以期於佛教團體生活中發揮所能，服務人群。

齊心共進

時值末法，世風險惡，本著法界佛教總會的宗旨，本會所屬之道場、機構，皆門戶開放，沒有人我、宗教、國籍等分別。凡願致力於仁義道德，追求真理，明心見性，利益人類的人士，皆歡迎至此，齊心努力研究，踏實修持學習，大家共同為利樂眾生而努力。

professional training for Buddhists around the world on both practical and theoretical levels, and transmitting the wisdom of the Buddha.

The Sangha Training Program gives monastics a solid foundation in Buddhist studies and practice, training them in the practical affairs of Buddhism and Sangha management. After graduation, students will be able to assume various responsibilities related to Buddhism in monasteries, institutions, and other settings. The program emphasizes a thorough knowledge of Buddhism, understanding of the scriptures, earnest cultivation, strict observance of precepts, and the development of a virtuous character, so that students will be able to propagate the Proper Dharma and perpetuate the Buddha's wisdom. The Laity Training Program offers courses to help laypeople develop correct views, study and practice the teachings, and understand monastic regulations and ceremonies, so that they will be able to contribute their abilities in Buddhist organizations.

Let Us Go Forward Together

In this Dharma-ending Age when the world is becoming increasingly dangerous and evil, the Dharma Realm Buddhist Association, in consonance with its guiding principles, opens the doors of its monasteries and centers to those of all religions and nationalities. Anyone who is devoted to humaneness, righteousness, virtue, and the pursuit of truth, and who wishes to understand him or herself and help humankind, is welcome to come study and practice with us. May we together bring benefit and happiness to all living beings.

宣化上人簡傳

東北時期

宣公上人，東北吉林省雙城縣人，民初戊午年農曆三月十六日生。俗姓白，名玉書，又名玉禧。父富海公，一生勤儉治家，以務農爲業。母胡太夫人，生前茹素念佛，數十年如一日；懷上人時，曾向佛菩薩祈願，生上人前夕，夢見阿彌陀佛大放光明，遂生上人。

上人生性沉默寡言，天賦俠義心腸，幼年即隨母親茹素念佛。年十一，見鄰居一死嬰，感生死事大，無常迅速，毅然有出家之志。十二歲，聞雙城王孝子 [上]常 [下]仁大師，盡孝得道，發願效法。懺悔過去不孝父母，決定每日早晚向父母叩頭認錯，以報親恩，自此漸以孝行見稱，人稱「白孝子」。

十五歲皈依 [上]常 [下]智老和尚爲師。同年入學，於四書五經、諸子百家、醫卜星相等，無不貫通。求學

A Biographical Sketch of the Venerable Master Hsuan Hua

Early Years in Manchuria

The Venerable Master was born in Shuangcheng County, Jilin Province, China, on the sixteenth day of the third lunar month in the year of *wuwu* at the beginning of the century. He was named Yushu (or Yuxi) Bai. His father, Fuhai Bai, was a hardworking, frugal farmer. His mother, whose maiden name was Hu, was vegetarian and recited the Buddha's name all her life. While carrying the Master, she prayed to the Buddhas and Bodhisattvas. The night before his birth, she saw Amitabha Buddha emitting brilliant light in her dream. Following that, the Master was born.

As a child, the Master was taciturn, but had a heroic spirit. He followed his mother in being vegetarian and reciting the Buddha's name. At the age of eleven, the sight of a dead infant made him aware of the great matter of birth and death, and he resolved to leave the home-life. At twelve, he heard of the filial practice of Filial Son Wang (Great Master Chang Ren) of Shuangcheng County and vowed to emulate him. The Master repented for not having been a good son and began to bow to his parents every morning and evening to repay their kindness. Because of his filial piety, he became known as Filial Son Bai.

At fifteen, he took refuge with the Venerable Master Chang Zhi. He also started school and mastered the Four Books, the Five Classics, the texts of various Chinese philosophers, and the fields of medicine, divination, astrology, and physiognomy. He

期間，參加道德會等慈善團體；又爲不識字者，講
《六祖壇經》、《金剛經》等；爲貧寒者，創辦義
務學校。

十九歲母親逝世，遂禮請三緣寺上常下智老和尚爲剃
度，法名安慈，字度輪。並披緇結廬於母親墓旁，
守孝期間，發十八大願，拜華嚴、禮淨懺、修禪定
、習教觀、日一食、夜不臥，功夫日純，得鄉里人
民之愛戴禮敬，其洗鍊精虔，感動諸佛菩薩、護法
龍天，故靈異之事多不勝數，人稱奇僧。

一日打坐，見六祖大師至茅棚，告曰：「將來你會
到西方，所遇之人無量無邊，教化眾生，如恆河沙
，不可悉數，此是西方佛法崛起之徵象。」言畢，
忽而不見。守孝期滿，隱居於長白山支脈彌陀洞內
修苦行。後回三緣寺，爲首座。居東北期間，觀機
逗教，點化迷蒙，濟世活人，感化無量龍蛇、狐狸
、鬼神，求皈受戒，改惡修善。

一九四六年，慕虛雲老和尚爲宗門泰斗，遂束裝就
道，前往參禮。途中備經艱苦，蹤跡遍及內陸各大

was active in the Virtue Society and other charity groups. He explained the *Sixth Patriarch's Sutra*, the *Vajra Sutra*, and other Sutras for the illiterate and started a free school for the poor.

At nineteen, after his mother's death, he requested Venerable Master Chang Zhi of Sanyuan (Three Conditions) Monastery to shave his head. He was given the Dharma names An Tse and To Lun. Donning monk's robes, he built a simple hut by his mother's grave and lived there for three years in observance of filial piety. During that period, he made eighteen great vows. He bowed to the *Flower Adornment Sutra*, repented and meditated, studied scriptures, ate only one meal a day, and slept sitting up at night. His skill in cultivation won the admiration of the villagers and evoked miraculous responses from the Buddhas, Bodhisattvas, and Dharma-protecting gods and dragons. He was regarded as an extraordinary monk.

One day while meditating, he saw the Sixth Patriarch come to his hut and tell him, "In the future you will go to the West and meet countless people. You will teach and transform beings as countless as the sands of the Ganges River. That will mark the beginning of the Buddhadharma in the West." With those words, the Sixth Patriarch vanished. The Master completed his filial observance and went to Changbai Mountain, where he dwelt in seclusion and practiced austerities at the Amitabha Cave. Later, he returned to Sanyuan Monastery and was made the head of the assembly. During his years in Manchuria, the Master taught people according to their potentials. He awakened those who were confused and saved many lives. Countless dragons, snakes, foxes, ghosts, and spirits reformed themselves upon receiving the refuges and precepts from him.

In 1946, the Master embarked on an arduous journey to pay homage to greatly revered Elder Master Hsu Yun. Along the

梵刹，一九四七年赴普陀山受具足戒，一九四八年
抵廣州曹溪南華寺，禮虛雲老和尚，受命任南華寺
戒律學院監學，後轉任教務主任。雲公觀其為法門
龍象，乃傳授法脈，賜法號宣化，遂為溈仰宗第九
代接法人，摩訶迦葉初祖傳承之第四十五代。

香江演教

一九四九年，叩別虛雲老和尚，赴香港弘法，闡揚
禪、教、律、密、淨五宗並重，打破門戶之見。並
重建古刹、印經造像，成立西樂園寺、慈興禪寺、
佛教講堂。居港十餘年間，應眾生懇請，普結法緣
，相續開講大乘經典多部，舉辦佛七、禪七、拜懺
等法會，又創辦《心法》雜誌等，終日為弘揚大法
而奔忙，使佛法興於香江。其間亦曾數度赴泰國、
緬甸等地，考察南傳佛教，志欲溝通大小乘，以團
結佛教力量。

大法西傳

一九五九年，師觀察西方機緣成熟，為將佛教之真
實義理傳播至世界各地，遂令弟子在美成立中美佛

way, he stayed at various renowned monasteries and received complete ordination at Mount Putuo in 1947. Arriving at Nanhua Monastery in Caoxi, Guangzhou, in 1948, he paid homage to Elder Master Hsu Yun. The Elder Master made him an instructor and later the Dean of Academic Affairs at Nanhua Vinaya Academy. He saw that the Master was an outstanding individual and transmitted the Dharma to him, giving him the Dharma name Hsuan Hua and making him the Ninth Patriarch of the Weiyang Sect, in the forty-fifth generation since the First Patriarch Mahakashyapa.

Teaching in Hong Kong

In 1949, the Master bid farewell to the Elder Master Yun and went to Hong Kong. In propagating the Dharma there, he emphasized all five schools of Buddhism (Chan, Doctrine, Vinaya, Esoteric, and Pure Land) and abolished sectarianism. He renovated old temples, printed Sutras, and constructed images. He founded Western Bliss Gardens Monastery, Cixing Chan Monastery, and the Buddhist Lecture Hall. For more than ten years, he created extensive Dharma-affinities with the people of Hong Kong. He expounded various Mahayana Sutras, organized recitation, meditation, and repentance sessions, and published the magazine *Hsin Fa (Mind Dharma)*. As a result of his energetic efforts, Buddhism flourished in Hong Kong. He also visited other countries such as Thailand and Burma to study Theravada Buddhism, in the hope of bringing the Mahayana and Theravada traditions together and uniting the forces of Buddhism.

The Dharma Goes West

In 1959, the Master saw that conditions were ripe in the West. For the sake of propagating Buddhism throughout the world,

教總會（法界佛教總會前身）。一九六一年，赴澳洲弘法一年，以機緣未熟，一九六二年返港。同年應美國佛教人士邀請，隻身赴美，樹正法幢於三藩市佛教講堂。初住無窗之潮濕地窖，猶如墳墓，故自號「墓中僧」。時值美蘇兩國有古巴飛彈危機之事，為求戰爭不起，世界和平，故絕食五星期。絕食畢，危機遂解。

一九六八年，成立暑假楞嚴講修班，有華盛頓州州立大學學生三十餘人，遠來學習佛法。結業後，美籍青年五人，懇求剃度出家，創美國佛教史始有僧相之記錄。隨著日益擴大的僧團，原有的佛教講堂不足敷用，遂於一九七〇年成立金山禪寺。一九七六年購置國際性大道場萬佛聖城。爾後金輪聖寺、金峰聖寺、華嚴聖寺、金佛聖寺、法界聖城等各分支道場相繼成立。上人不遺餘力致力於弘法、譯經、教育等事業，廣建道場、培植人才、訂立宗旨。集四眾之真誠，盡未來際劫，遍虛空法界，光大如來正法家業。

在弘法方面，上人教導弟子天天參禪打坐、念佛、

he instructed his disciples to establish the Sino-American Buddhist Association (renamed the Dharma Realm Buddhist Association) in the United States. In 1961 he propagated the Dharma in Australia for one year. Since the conditions were not ripe there, he returned to Hong Kong in 1962. Later that year, at the invitation of Buddhists in America, the Master traveled alone to the United States and raised the banner of the Proper Dharma at the Buddhist Lecture Hall in San Francisco. Living in a damp, windowless basement that resembled a grave, he called himself "The Monk in the Grave." During the Cuban Missile Crisis, the Master observed a five-week fast to pray for peace. By the end of his fast, the crisis was over.

During the Shurangama Study and Practice Summer Session in 1968, over thirty students from the University of Washington in Seattle went to San Francisco to study with the Master. At the end of the session, five of them requested permission to enter the monastic life. That was the beginning of the Sangha in the history of American Buddhism. The Buddhist Lecture Hall became too small for the growing Sangha. Gold Mountain Dhyana Monastery was founded in 1970, and the City of Ten Thousand Buddhas was established in 1976 as an international monastic community. Later various branches were founded, such as Gold Wheel Monastery, Gold Summit Monastery, Avatamsaka Monastery, Gold Buddha Monastery, and the City of the Dharma Realm. The Master devoted himself to the propagation of the Dharma, the translation of the Buddhist Canon, and education. He established monasteries, helped people develop their talents, and set forth principles. He led the fourfold assembly in working to spread Proper Dharma throughout the Dharma Realm.

The Master taught his disciples to meditate, recite the Buddha's name, practice repentance, study the Sutras, and observe the

拜懺、研究經典、嚴持戒律、日中一食、衣不離體
，和合共住，互相砥礪，在西方建立行持正法之僧
團，以圖匡扶正教，令正法久住。又開放萬佛聖城
爲國際性宗教中心，提倡融合南北傳佛教，團結世
界宗教，大家互相學習，溝通合作，共同追求眞理
，爲世界和平而努力。

「只要我有一口氣在，就要講經說法。」上人講經
說法，深入淺出，數十年如一日。並極力栽培四眾
弘法人才，觀機逗教，化導東西方善信。多次率團
至各大學，及世界各國弘法訪問，以期引導眾生改
惡向善，開啓本有智慧。

在譯經方面，現已有百餘本譯爲英文，中英文雙語
佛書也陸續在出版中。另有西班牙文、越南文、日
文等譯本，法文、德文譯本則指日可待。預計將《
大藏經》譯成各國文字，使佛法傳遍寰宇。近三十
年歷史的《金剛菩提海》雜誌先是純英文版，後逐
漸演變爲中英對照月刊，今共發行了三百多期。至
於中文佛書更是接踵而出，不下百部，多種語言之

precepts. He taught them to eat only one meal a day (at midday) and to always wear the precept sash. He taught them to dwell in harmony and to encourage each other. He established a Sangha that practices the Proper Dharma in the West, in the hope of restoring orthodox Buddhism and keeping it alive in the world forever. The Master founded the City of Ten Thousand Buddhas as an international spiritual community where followers of different traditions of Buddhism and religions of the world can come together to learn, communicate, and work together for the sake of truth and world peace.

"As long as I have a single breath left, I will explain the Sutras and speak the Dharma." The Master expounded the Sutras and Dharma daily for several decades, explaining profound principles in a way that made them easy to understand. He also trained his monastic and lay disciples to explain the teachings. Always adjusting his teaching to the individual and the situation, he transformed both Eastern and Western disciples. He led numerous delegations to teach the Dharma in universities and nations around the world, inspiring people to turn toward goodness and discover their innate wisdom.

To date, over a hundred volumes of the Master's explanations of the scriptures have been translated into English, and some have been published in bilingual Chinese/English format. A number of Spanish, Vietnamese, and Japanese translations have been published, and French and German versions will soon be available. The Master's aim is to translate the entire Buddhist Canon into all languages so that the Dharma will be readily accessible worldwide. The monthly journal *Vajra Bodhi Sea* was first published nearly thirty years ago in English only. Later it adopted a bilingual Chinese/English format, and to date over 300 issues have been published. Over a hundred Chinese Buddhist texts have also been published. Audio and video tapes

錄音帶、錄影帶亦不斷發行中，以爲眾生聞法修行之良箴。

在教育方面，萬佛聖城設有育良小學、培德中學、法界佛教大學、僧伽居士訓練班等教育機構。分支道場於周末、周日亦附設佛學班、中文學校。這些融入佛教精神的教育機構以孝悌忠信、禮義廉恥八德，爲做人的基礎。以大公無私、慈悲喜捨爲究竟目標。男女分校，提倡義務教學，培養品格高尚、具備眞知灼見的人才，以期利益世界人類。

法輪無盡

上人一生大公無私，發願代眾生受一切苦難，將己身一切福樂迴向法界眾生，難行能行，難忍能忍，其堅貞之志節，堪爲疾風中之勁燭，烈火內之精金。上人曾撰一聯以明其志：

> 凍死不攀緣，
> 餓死不化緣，
> 窮死不求緣；
> 隨緣不變，不變隨緣，
> 抱定我們三大宗旨。

in several languages are currently being produced, so that people may hear the Dharma and cultivate accordingly.

In the area of education, the Master established Instilling Goodness Elementary School, Developing Virtue Secondary School, Dharma Realm Buddhist University, and the Sangha and Laity Training Programs at the City of Ten Thousand Buddhas. Many of the branch monasteries of the Dharma Realm Buddhist Association have weekend classes in Buddhism and Chinese for children as well. These educational programs integrate the teachings of Buddhism with the eight virtues of filiality, fraternal respect, loyalty, trustworthiness, propriety, righteousness, incorruptibility, and a sense of shame. Their ultimate aim is to encourage students to develop a public-minded spirit, kindness, compassion, joy, and charity. Boys and girls study separately, and the faculty of volunteer teachers guides students to develop into capable individuals with integrity and wisdom who will be able to benefit humankind.

The Infinite Dharma Wheel
The Master's life was one of total selflessness. He vowed to take the suffering and hardships of all living beings upon himself, and to dedicate to them all the blessings and happiness that he himself ought to enjoy. He practiced what was difficult to practice and endured what was difficult to endure. No amount of hardship could deter him from fulfilling his lofty resolves. He composed a verse expressing his principles:

> Freezing, we do not scheme.
> Starving, we do not beg.
> Dying of poverty, we ask for nothing.
> According with conditions, we do not change.
> Not changing, we accord with conditions.
> We adhere firmly to our three great principles.

> 捨命爲佛事，
>
> 造命爲本事，
>
> 正命爲僧事；
>
> 即事明理，明理即事，
>
> 推行祖師一脈心傳。

上人又堅守一生奉行之六大條款：「不爭、不貪、不求、不自私、不自利、不打妄語」，利益群生；其慈悲智慧之教化，捨己爲人、以身作則之精神，令無數人眞誠改過，走向清淨光明之菩提大道。

眾生障深福薄，一九九五年一代聖人遽爾示寂，娑婆眾生頓失依怙；然而上人之一生，即是一部法界的華嚴大經，雖示現涅槃，而恒轉無盡法輪不留痕跡，從虛空來，回到虛空去。弟子眾等唯有恪遵師教，抱定宗旨，在菩薩道上精進不懈，以期報上人浩瀚之深恩於萬一。

We renounce our lives to do the Buddha's work.
We take the responsibility to mold our own destinies.
We rectify our lives to fulfill the Sanghan's role.
Encountering specific matters,
  we understand the principles.
Understanding the principles,
  we apply them in specific matters.
We carry on the single pulse of
  the Patriarchs' mind-transmission.

Through his unwavering, lifelong maintenance of the six guiding principles of not contending, not being greedy, not seeking, not being selfish, not pursuing personal advantage, and not lying, he brought benefit to many. Teaching with wisdom and compassion, dedicating himself to serving others, and acting as a model for others, he influenced countless people to change their faults and to walk upon the pure, bright path to enlightenment.

Deep are the obstructions of living beings and scanty are their blessings, for this Sage manifested entry into stillness in 1995 and we of the Saha World suddenly lost our refuge. Yet the Venerable Master's life is actually an enactment of the great Sutra of the Dharma Realm—the *Flower Adornment Sutra*. Although he has manifested entry into Nirvana, he constantly turns the infinite Dharma wheel. He came from space, and to space he returned without leaving a trace. His disciples must carefully follow their teacher's instructions, hold fast to their principles, honor the Buddha's regulations, and advance with vigor toward Bodhi so that they may repay a tiny fraction of the Venerable Master's boundless and profound grace.

287

宣化上人十八大願

一、願盡虛空、遍法界、十方三世一切菩薩等，若有一未成佛時，我誓不取正覺。

二、願盡虛空、遍法界、十方三世一切緣覺等，若有一未成佛時，我誓不取正覺。

三、願盡虛空、遍法界、十方三世一切聲聞等，若有一未成佛時，我誓不取正覺。

四、願三界諸天人等，若有一未成佛時，我誓不取正覺。

五、願十方世界一切人等，若有一未成佛時，我誓不取正覺。

The Eighteen Great Vows of Venerable Master Hsuan Hua

1. I vow that as long as there is a single Bodhisattva in the three periods of time throughout the ten directions of the Dharma Realm, to the very ends of empty space, who has not accomplished Buddhahood, I too will not attain the right enlightenment.

2. I vow that as long as there is a single Pratyekabuddha in the three periods of time throughout the ten directions of the Dharma Realm, to the very ends of empty space, who has not accomplished Buddhahood, I too will not attain the right enlightenment.

3. I vow that as long as there is a single Shravaka in the three periods of time throughout the ten directions of the Dharma Realm, to the very ends of empty space, who has not accomplished Buddhahood, I too will not attain the right enlightenment.

4. I vow that as long as there is a single god in the Triple Realm who has not accomplished Buddhahood, I too will not attain the right enlightenment.

5. I vow that as long as there is a single human being in the worlds of the ten directions who has not accomplished Buddhahood, I too will not attain the right enlightenment.

六、願天、人、一切阿修羅等，若有一未成佛時，
我誓不取正覺。

七、願一切畜生界等，若有一未成佛時，我誓不取
正覺。

八、願一切餓鬼界等，若有一未成佛時，我誓不取
正覺。

九、願一切地獄界等，若有一未成佛，或地獄不空
時，我誓不取正覺。

十、願凡是三界諸天、仙、人、阿修羅，飛潛動植
、靈界龍畜、鬼神等眾，曾經皈依我者，若有
一未成佛時，我誓不取正覺。

十一、願將我所應享受一切福樂，悉皆迴向，普施
法界眾生。

十二、願將法界眾生所有一切苦難，悉皆與我一人
代受。

6. I vow that as long as there is a single asura who has not accomplished Buddhahood, I too will not attain the right enlightenment.

7. I vow that as long as there is a single animal who has not accomplished Buddhahood, I too will not attain the right enlightenment.

8. I vow that as long as there is a single hungry ghost who has not accomplished Buddhahood, I too will not attain the right enlightenment.

9. I vow that as long as there is a single hell-dweller who has not accomplished Buddhahood, I too will not attain the right enlightenment.

10. I vow that as long as there is a single god, immortal, human, asura, air-bound or water-bound creature, animate creature or inanimate object, or a single dragon, beast, ghost, or spirit, and so forth, of the spiritual realm that has taken refuge with me and has not accomplished Buddhahood, I too will not attain the right enlightenment.

11. I vow to fully dedicate all blessings and bliss which I myself ought to receive and enjoy to all living beings of the Dharma Realm.

12. I vow to fully take upon myself all the sufferings and hardships of all the living beings in the Dharma Realm.

十三、願分靈無數，普入一切不信佛法眾生心，令
　　其改惡向善，悔過自新，皈依三寶，究竟作
　　佛。

十四、願一切眾生，見我面，乃至聞我名，悉發菩
　　提心，速得成佛道。

十五、願恪遵佛制，實行日中一食。

十六、願覺諸有情，普攝群機。

十七、願此生即得五眼六通，飛行自在。

十八、願一切求願，必獲滿足。

結云：

> 眾生無邊誓願度
> 煩惱無盡誓願斷
> 法門無量誓願學
> 佛道無上誓願成

13. I vow to manifest innumerable bodies as a means to gain access into the minds of living beings throughout the universe who do not believe in the Buddhadharma, causing them to correct their faults and tend toward wholesomeness, repent of their errors and start anew, take refuge in the Triple Jewel, and ultimately accomplish Buddhahood.

14. I vow that all living beings who see my face or even hear my name will bring forth the Bodhi resolve and quickly accomplish Buddhahood.

15. I vow to respectfully observe the Buddha's instructions and cultivate the practice of eating only one meal per day.

16. I vow to enlighten all sentient beings, universally responding to the multitudes of differing potentials.

17. I vow to obtain the five eyes, the six spiritual powers, and the freedom of being able to fly in this very life.

18. I vow that all of my vows will certainly be fulfilled.

Conclusion:

> I vow to save the innumerable living beings.
> I vow to eradicate the inexhaustible afflictions.
> I vow to study the illimitable Dharma-doors.
> I vow to accomplish the unsurpassed Buddha Way.

宇宙白

此首「宇宙白」，乃一九七二年二月十五日宣公上人所作。當時金山禪寺舉行誦念「六字大明咒」法會，四眾弟子，二十四小時不停地虔誠持誦，無有倦怠，以祈禱世界和平。待七天法會圓滿之後，上人有感而作此首「宇宙白」。「宇宙白」表示整個宇宙都清淨了，沒有染污了，都變成光明潔白的了。但要宇宙沒有染污，必須勇猛精進，從「流血汗，不休息」做起。

冰天雪地
無數條小蟲凍斃　且蟄眠
靜裏觀察　動中審諦
龍爭虎鬥常遊戲
鬼哭神嚎幻化奇
真實義絕言　不思議　當進趨
大小泯　內外非
微塵遍　法界周
團圓個圓融　互相無礙

White Universe

The Venerable Master composed the poem "White Universe" on February 15, 1972, during a session for recitation of the Six-syllable Great Bright Mantra (Om mani padme hum) at Gold Mountain Dhyana Monastery. The fourfold assembly of disciples sincerely recited around the clock without fatigue, praying for world peace. Upon completion of the seven-day session, the Venerable Master was inspired to compose this poem. "White Universe" signifies that the entire universe has been purified, so that it is luminous and immaculately white. In order for the universe to be free from defilement, we must cultivate vigorously and begin by "sparing neither blood nor sweat, and never pausing to rest."

Ice in the sky, snow on the ground.
Numberless tiny bugs die in the cold
    or sleep in hibernation.
In the midst of stillness you should contemplate,
    and within movement you should investigate.
Dragons spar and tigers wrestle in continual playful sport;
Ghosts cry and spirits wail,
    their illusory transformations strange.
Ultimate truth transcends words;
Not thought about or talked about,
    you ought to advance with haste.
With great and small destroyed, with no inside or out,
It pervades every mote of dust
    and encompasses the Dharma Realm,

雙拳打破虛空蓋
一口吞盡剎海源
大慈悲普度
流血汗　不休息

Complete, whole, and perfectly fused,
    interpenetrating without obstruction.
With two clenched fists, shatter the covering of
    empty space.
In one mouthful, swallow the source of
    seas of Buddhalands.
With great compassion rescue all,
Sparing neither blood nor sweat, and never pause to rest!

迴向偈

願以此功德　　莊嚴佛淨土
上報四重恩　　下濟三途苦
若有見聞者　　悉發菩提心
盡此一報身　　同生極樂國

Verse of Transference

May the merit and virtue accrued from this work
Adorn the Buddhas' Pure Lands,
Repaying the four kinds of kindness above
And aiding those suffering in the paths below.
May those who see and hear of this
All bring forth the resolve for Bodhi
And, when this retribution body is over,
Be born together in the Land of Ultimate Bliss.

南無護法韋馱菩薩
Namo Dharma Protector Weitou Bodhisattva

DHARMA REALM BUDDHIST ASSOCIATION
BUDDHIST TEXT TRANSLATION SOCIETY
PUBLICATIONS

法界佛教總會
佛經翻譯委員會

Lectures by the Venerable Master Hsuan Hua
宣化上人法音宣流

Chinese/English Buddhist Books & Tapes
中/英文佛經叢書、錄音帶目錄

1

宣化上人經典淺釋 (中文佛書)	冊	版本
◆ 大方廣佛華嚴經淺釋	23	平裝
◆ 華嚴經‧普賢菩薩行願品淺釋	1	平裝
◆ 大方廣佛華嚴經疏序淺釋	1	平裝
◆ 大佛頂首楞嚴經淺釋	2	精裝
◆ 楞嚴經‧大勢至菩薩念佛圓通章淺釋	1	平裝
◆ 楞嚴經‧五十陰魔淺釋	1	精裝
◆ 楞嚴經‧四種清淨明誨淺釋	1	平裝
◆ 妙法蓮華經淺釋	2	精裝
◆ 法華經‧安樂行品淺釋	1	精裝
◆ 法華經‧觀世音菩薩普門品淺釋	1	平裝
◆ 佛說四十二章經淺釋	1	精裝
◆ 金剛般若波羅蜜經淺釋	1	精裝
◆ 般若波羅蜜多心經非台頌解	1	精裝
◆ 藥師琉璃光如來本願功德經淺釋	1	精裝
◆ 佛說阿彌陀經淺釋	1	精裝
◆ 地藏菩薩本願經淺釋	1	精裝
◆ 大悲心陀羅尼經淺釋	1	精裝
◆ 六祖法寶壇經淺釋	2	精裝
◆ 永嘉大師證道歌淺釋	1	平裝
◆ 永嘉大師證道歌詮釋 (附圖)	1	平裝
◆ 大乘百法明門論淺釋	1	平裝
◆ 佛遺教經淺釋	1	平裝

宣化上人開示 (中文佛書)

	冊	版本
◆ ᴸ宣ᶠ化老和尚偈讚歌詠專輯 (彩色盒裝)	1	精裝
◆ 宣化上人開示錄	6	平裝
◆ 宣化上人開示錄 (一九九三訪台開示)	1	平裝
◆ 人生要義 (革新版)	1	平裝
◆ 佛教新紀元 (歐洲弘法記)	1	平裝
◆ 春日蓮華	1	平裝
◆ 春日蓮華 (日文版)	1	平裝
◆ 宣化上人法語開示	1	平裝
◆ 教育救國	1	平裝
◆ 道德救國	1	平裝
◆ 十法界不離一念心	1	平裝
◆ 十法界不離一念心 (日文版)	1	平裝
◆ 水鏡回天錄 (正文)	2	精裝
◆ 水鏡回天錄白話解 (帝王篇)	1	平裝
◆ 照妖鏡 (宣化上人經典開示選輯1)	1	平裝
◆ 菩提本無樹 (宣化上人經典開示選輯2)	1	平裝
◆ 地獄不空 (宣化上人經典開示選輯3)	1	平裝
◆ 千手千眼 (宣化上人經典開示選輯4)	1	平裝
◆ 世紀末鐘聲 (宣化上人語錄1)	1	平裝

事蹟傳記

◆ 宣化上人事蹟	1	平裝
◆ ᴸ宣ᶠ化老和尚略傳	1	平裝

其他中文佛書	冊	版本
◆ 大方廣佛華嚴經 (經文/注音/盒裝)	6	袖珍
◆ 大佛頂首楞嚴經 (經文/注音)	1	袖珍
◆ 楞嚴咒・大悲咒・十小咒 (護照本)	1	平裝
◆ 法滅盡經 (經文)	1	平裝
◆ 誌公禪師因果經 (經文)	1	精裝
◆ 普賢菩薩行願品等六經咒 (經文)	1	平裝
◆ 梵網經菩薩戒本持犯集證類編	1	平裝
◆ 優婆塞戒經講錄	1	平裝
◆ 學佛行儀、五戒表解合訂本	1	平裝
◆ 禪海十珍	1	平裝
◆ 參禪要旨 (虛雲老和尚開示)	1	平裝
◆ 佛教精進者的日記	2	平裝
◆ 修行者的消息	1	平裝
◆ 人之根 (注音版)	1	平裝

中英雙語佛書 Bilingual Chinese/English Buddhist Books	冊 No. of Vols	版本 Edition
◆ 大方廣佛華嚴經疏序淺釋 Flower Adornment (Avatamsaka) Sutra Preface	1	平裝 softcover
◆ 楞嚴經五十陰魔淺釋 The Shurangama Sutra: The Fifty Skandha-Demon States	1	精裝 hardcover
◆ 佛說四十二章經淺釋 The Sutra in Forty-two Sections Spoken by the Buddha	1	精裝 hardcover
◆ 宣化上人開示錄 Ven. Master Hua's Talks on Dharma, Vol. 1-9	9	平裝 softcover
◆ 宣化上人開示錄 (一九九三訪臺開示) Ven. Master Hua's Talks on Dharma during the 1993 Trip to Taiwan	1	平裝 softcover

中英雙語佛書 Bilingual Chinese/English Buddhist Books	冊 No. of Vols	版本 Edition
◆ 十法界不離一念心 The Ten Dharma Realms Are Not Beyond A Single Thought	1	平裝 softcover
◆ 正法的代表 (袖珍本) A Sure Sign of the Proper Dharma	1	平裝 softcover
◆ 百年大事渾如夢 (袖珍本) The Great Events of One Hundred Years Are Hazy As If a Dream	1	平裝 softcover
◆ 皈依的真義 (袖珍本) The True Meaning of Taking Refuge	1	平裝 softcover
◆ 訪歐開示 Dharma Talks in Europe	1	平裝 softcover
◆ 達摩祖師西來意 (注音附圖/老少咸宜) The Intention of Patriarch Bodhidharma's Coming from the West (Appropriate for children and adults. Generously illustrated with black and white Chinese brush drawings.)	1	平裝 softcover
◆ 虛雲老和尚畫傳集 Pictorial Biography of the Ven. Master Hsu Yun	1	精裝 hardcover
◆ 大龜王 (兒童彩色佛書/注音) The Giant Turtle (Buddhist story for young readers)	1	平裝 softcover
◆ 宣化老和尚追思紀念專集 (一) In Memory of the Ven. Master Hua's, Vol. 1	1	精裝 hardcover
◆ 宣化老和尚追思紀念專集 (二) In Memory of the Ven. Master Hua's, Vol. 2	1	精裝 hardcover
◆ 宣化老和尚示寂週年暨 萬佛聖城成立廿週年紀念專集 In Memory of the First Anniversary of the Nirvana of Ven. Master Hsuan Hua and the 20th Anniversary of the City of 10,000 Buddhas	1	精裝 hardcover
◆ 萬佛聖城成立廿週年特刊 Celebrating the 20th Anniversary of the City of 10,000 Buddhas	2	平裝 softcover

中英雙語佛書冊 **Bilingual Chinese/English** **Buddhist Books**	冊 No. of Vols	版本 Edition
◆ 萬佛聖城日誦儀規 City of Ten Thousand Buddhas Recitation Handbook	1	平裝 softcover
◆ 初一、十五佛前大供儀規 The Meal Offering Before the Buddhas for First and Fifteen of Lunar Month	1	平裝 softcover
◆ 大悲懺本 Great Compassion Repentance	1	平裝 softcover
◆ 華嚴經普賢行願品・華嚴普賢行願懺儀・ 華嚴經疏序 (合訂本) Flower Adornment Dharmas: Conduct and Vows of Universal Worthy, Flower Adornment Repentance, Flower Adornment Preface (a set)	1	精裝 hardcover

---

Vajra Bodhi Sea

Vajra Bodhi Sea is a monthly journal of orthodox Buddhism which has been published by the Dharma Realm Buddhist Association, formerly known as the Sino-American Buddhist Association, since 1970. Each issue contains the most recent translations of the Buddhist canon by the Buddhist Text Translation Society. Also included in each issue are a biography of a great Patriarch of Buddhism from the ancient past, sketches of the lives of contemporary monastics and lay-followers around the world, articles on practice, and other material. The journal is bilingual, Chinese and English, 48 pages in an 8 1/2" by 11" format. ISSN 0507-6986. Single issues, NT100.00. One year subscription, NT1200.00; three years, NT3000.00. (Postage is included in the subscription fee.)

月刊 (中英版)	新台幣
萬佛城月刊金剛菩提海雜誌 (單行本)	100 元
萬佛城月刊金剛菩提海雜誌 (訂閱一年)	1200 元
萬佛城月刊金剛菩提海雜誌 (訂閱二年)	2400 元
萬佛城月刊金剛菩提海雜誌 (訂閱三年)	3000 元

宣化上人經典淺釋(中文錄音帶)	卷	包裝	新台幣
◆ 華嚴經‧普賢行願品淺釋	*18	盒裝	900 元
◆ 華嚴經‧淨行品淺釋	12	盒裝	600 元
◆ 大方廣佛華嚴經疏序淺釋	*8	盒裝	400 元
◆ 大佛頂首楞嚴經淺釋	*120	盒裝	6000 元
◆ 楞嚴經‧四種清淨明誨淺釋	*4	盒裝	200 元
◆ 楞嚴經‧大勢至菩薩念佛圓通章淺釋	4	盒裝	250 元
◆ 法華經‧安樂行品淺釋	9	盒裝	450 元
◆ 法華經‧觀世音菩薩普門品淺釋	15	盒裝	750 元
◆ 佛說四十二章經淺釋	*6	盒裝	300 元
◆ 金剛般若波羅蜜經淺釋	*14	盒裝	700 元
◆ 般若波羅蜜多心經非台頌解	*8	盒裝	400 元
◆ 佛說阿彌陀經淺釋	14	盒裝	700 元
◆ 六祖法寶壇經淺釋	*24	盒裝	1200 元
◆ 永嘉大師證道歌淺釋	11	盒裝	550 元
◆ 勸發菩提心文淺釋 (1979 年)	5	盒裝	250 元
◆ 勸發菩提心文淺釋 (1985 年)	6	盒裝	300 元
◆ 大乘百法明門論淺釋	*5	盒裝	250 元
◆ 佛遺教經淺釋	*9	盒裝	450 元

*附書

事蹟傳記 (中文錄音帶)

◆ 佛陀十大弟子傳	3	盒裝	150 元
◆ 高僧傳	22	盒裝	1000 元

宣化上人開示(中文錄音帶)	卷	包裝	新台幣
◆ 十法界不離一念心	3	盒裝	150 元
◆ 佛七精華錄	5	盒裝	250 元
◆ 念佛法門到彼岸	3	盒裝	150 元
◆ 禪 (開示)	3	盒裝	150 元
◆ 觀音菩薩的智慧鑰匙	4	盒裝	200 元
◆ 救世界教育的靈丹	3	盒裝	150 元
◆ 正法的震撼—一九八八年臺灣弘法專集	12	盒裝	600 元
◆ 宣化上人開示錄（一） 一九八八年馬來西亞弘法專集	4	盒裝	200 元
◆ 宣化上人開示錄（二） 美加地區等弘法專集	6	盒裝	300 元
◆ 宣化上人開示錄（四） 一九八九年臺灣弘法專集	7	盒裝	350 元
◆ 宣化上人開示錄（五） 一九九〇年臺灣弘法專集	6	盒裝	3000 元
◆ 宣化上人開示錄（六） 一九九三年訪臺開示	5	盒裝	250 元
◆ 宣化上人開示錄 一九九四年於美國之開示	7	單片	100 元
◆ 莫道念佛容易事	1	單片	100 元
◆ 念經妙處多	1	單片	100 元
◆ 供養三寶的規矩	1	單片	100 元
◆ 如何增長智慧	1	單片	100 元
◆ 修行人要認識境界	1	單片	100 元
◆ 莫自稱居士	1	單片	100 元
◆ 夢裏說夢	1	單片	100 元
◆ 為什麼要放生	1	單片	100 元
◆ 莫道念佛容易事 (國閩版)	1	單片	150 元
◆ 對面不識觀世音 (國閩版)	1	單片	150 元

法界佛教總會
Dharma Realm Buddhist Association Branches
Home Page: http:\\www.drba.org
Main Branch:

萬佛聖城
The City of Ten Thousand Buddhas
P.O. Box 217, Talmage, CA 95481-0217 U.S.A.
Tel: (707) 462-0939   Fax: (707) 462-0949

國際譯經學院 The International Translation Institute
1777 Murchison Drive, Burlingame, CA 94010-4504 U.S.A.
Tel: (650) 692-5912   Fax: (650) 692-5056

法界宗教研究院 (柏克萊寺)
Institute for World Religions (at Berkeley Buddhist Monastery)
2304 McKinley Avenue, Berkeley, CA 94703 U.S.A.
Tel: (510) 848-3440   Fax: (510) 548-4551

金山聖寺 Gold Mountain Monastery
800 Sacramento Street, San Francisco, CA 94108 U.S.A.
Tel: (415) 421-6117   Fax: (415) 788-6001

金聖寺 Gold Sage Monastery
11455 Clayton Road, San Jose, CA 95127 U.S.A.
Tel: (408) 923-7243   Fax: (408) 923-1064

法界聖城 The City of the Dharma Realm
1029 West Capitol Avenue, West Sacramento, CA 95691 U.S.A.
Tel/Fax: (916) 374-8268

金輪聖寺 Gold Wheel Monastery
235 North Avenue 58, Los Angeles, CA 90042 U.S.A.
Tel/Fax: (323) 258-6668

長堤聖寺 Long Beach Monastery
3361 East Ocean Boulevard, Long Beach, CA 90803 U.S.A.
Tel/Fax: (562) 438-8902

福祿壽聖寺 Blessings, Prosperity, and Longevity Monastery
4140 Long Beach Boulevard, Long Beach, CA 90807 U.S.A.
Tel/Fax: (562) 595-4966

華嚴精舍 Avatamsaka Hermitage
11721 Beall Mountain Road, Potomac, MD 20854-1128 U.S.A.
Tel/Fax: (301) 299-3693

金峰聖寺 Gold Summit Monastery
233 First Avenue West, Seattle, WA 98119 U.S.A.
Tel/Fax: (206) 217-9320

金佛聖寺 Gold Buddha Monastery
248 E. 11th Avenue, Vancouver, B.C. V5T 2C3 Canada
Tel/Fax: (604) 709-0248

華嚴聖寺 Avatamsaka Monastery
1009 Fourth Avenue S.W. Calgary, AB T2P 0K8 Canada
Tel/Fax: (403) 234-0644

法界佛教總會駐華辦事處（法界佛教印經會）
Dharma Realm Buddhist Books Distribution Society
臺灣省臺北市忠孝東路六段 85 號 11 樓
Tel: (02) 2786-3022, 2786-2474   Fax: (02) 2786-2674

法界聖寺 Dharma Realm Monastery
臺灣省高雄縣六龜鄉興龍村東溪山莊 20 號
Tel: (07) 689-3713   Fax: (07) 689-3870

彌陀聖寺 Amitabha Monastery
臺灣省花蓮縣壽豐鄉池南村四健會 7 號
Tel: (03) 865-1956 Fax:(03) 865-3426

紫雲洞觀音寺 Tze Yun Tung Temple
Batu 5 1/2, Jalan Sungai Besi, Salak Selatan, 57100 Kuala Lumpur, Malaysia
Tel: (03)782-6560   Fax:(03) 780-1272

佛教講堂 Buddhist Lecture Hall
香港跑馬地黃泥涌道 31 號 11 樓
31 Wong Nei Chong Road, Top Floor, Happy Valley, Hong Kong, China.

宣化上人開示錄（九）

西曆二〇〇一年一月二日・中英版平裝
佛曆三〇二七年十二月八日・釋迦牟尼佛成道日・初版

發行人　法界佛教總會
出　版　法界佛教總會・佛經翻譯委員會・法界佛教大學
地　址　**Dharma Realm Buddhist Association &**
　　　　The City of Ten Thousand Buddhas
　　　　2001 Talmage Road, Talmage, CA 95481-0217 U.S.A.
　　　　電話: (707) 462-0939　傳真: (707) 462-0949

The International Translation Institute
1777 Murchison Drive Burlingame, CA 94010-4504 U.S.A.
電話: (650) 692-5912　傳真: (650) 692-5056

倡　印　法界佛教總會駐華辦事處（法界佛教印經會）
　　　　臺灣省臺北市忠孝東路六段 85 號 11 樓
　　　　電話: (02) 2786-3022, 2786-2474　傳真: (02) 2786-2674
　　　　劃撥帳號:1321798-5　帳戶:張淑彤

法界文教基金會
臺灣省高雄縣六龜鄉興龍村東溪山莊 20 號
電話: (07) 689-3713

ISBN 0-88139-858-6

●佛典所在，即佛所在，請恭敬尊重，廣為流通。